D1607766

# Intercultural Communication

# Intercultural
# Communication

## *Building a Global Community*

**Fay Patel**
**Mingsheng Li**
**Prahalad Sooknanan**

 SAGE    www.sagepublications.com
Los Angeles • London • New Delhi • Singapore • Washington DC

*First published in 2011 by*

**SAGE Publications India Pvt Ltd**
B1/I-1 Mohan Cooperative Industrial Area
Mathura Road, New Delhi 110 044, India
*www.sagepub.in*

**SAGE Publications Inc**
2455 Teller Road
Thousand Oaks, California 91320, USA

**SAGE Publications Ltd**
1 Oliver's Yard, 55 City Road
London EC1Y 1SP, United Kingdom

**SAGE Publications Asia-Pacific Pte Ltd**
33 Pekin Street
#02-01 Far East Square
Singapore 048763

Published by Vivek Mehra for SAGE Publications India Pvt Ltd, typeset in 10.5/12.5 pt Adobe Garamond Pro by Star Compugraphics Private Limited, Delhi and printed at Chaman Enterprises, New Delhi.

**Library of Congress Cataloging-in-Publication Data**

Patel, Fay.
    Intercultural communication: building a global community/Fay Patel, Mingsheng Li, Prahalad Sooknanan.
        p. cm.
    Includes bibliographical references and index.

1. Intercultural communication. 2. Globalization–Social aspects. I. Li, Mingsheng, 1957- II. Sooknanan, Prahalad. III. Title.

HM1211.P38        303.48'2—dc22        2011        2011006872

**ISBN:** 978-81-321-0634-0 (HB)

**The SAGE Team:** Elina Majumdar, Arpita Dasgupta, Amrita Saha and Deepti Saxena

This book is dedicated to all those who strive for social justice in their day-to-day lives and who continue to demonstrate patience, tolerance and good faith in an effort to build a global community that values respect and dignity. It is our hope that in all intercultural communication interactions around the globe, respect and dignity will become the norm for future generations.

\*\*\*

I am grateful to God for the courage to pursue what is just and to strengthen my belief and faith in the goodness of all people. I thank my husband Feisal and our son Farhaan for their ongoing encouragement and support of my work in the area of intercultural communication and in the promotion of cultural diversity awareness. Without them at my side and without their unconditional love and patience, it would not have been possible to realize this dream and to complete the enormous task of writing a book about building global communities.

*Fay (Feiziya) Patel*

I express my gratitude to my wife Huaiyu Wang and daughter Zheng Li for their strong support, understanding and sacrifice. They came from China to be reunited with me in Australia when I did my doctoral studies and later we migrated to New Zealand.

*Mingsheng Li*

I particularly wish to thank my wife Valerie, daughter Shiveta and son Shival for their support and love and their patience during the years I studied in Ohio in the United States of America where I completed my doctoral studies.

*Prahalad Sooknanan*

*Thank you for choosing a SAGE product! If you have any comment,*
*observation or feedback, I would like to personally hear from you.*
*Please write to me at* <u>contactceo@sagepub.in</u>

—Vivek Mehra, Managing Director and CEO,
SAGE Publications India Pvt Ltd, New Delhi

**Bulk Sales**

SAGE India offers special discounts for purchase of books in bulk.
We also make available special imprints and excerpts from our
books on demand.

For orders and enquiries, write to us at

*Marketing Department*
*SAGE Publications India Pvt Ltd*
*B1/I-1, Mohan Cooperative Industrial Area*
*Mathura Road, Post Bag 7*
*New Delhi 110044, India*
E-mail us at <u>marketing@sagepub.in</u>

*Get to know more about SAGE, be invited to SAGE events, get on*
*our mailing list. Write today to* <u>marketing@sagepub.in</u>

This book is also available as an e-book.

# Contents

# Foreword

The authors of this book have embraced a challenging but very important task of providing insights into intercultural communication in ways that honour powerful and deeply held views from multiple cultures. Each of the three authors celebrate in these pages the struggles they have encountered in their own developmental journey, and the message of this work is stronger for it.

The book rightly points to the growing realization that freely-available education for all opens doors to new ways of seeing and being in the world. Correctly, the authors describe how earlier generations valued education, realizing its salience as a means by which social conditions could be improved and familial aspirations might be met. However, Patel, Li and Sooknanan also rightly show how education is more than about just opening the door to better jobs and income. These are important but, in a rapidly globalizing world, not enough. Also essential is education that creates an improved person, one more sophisticated in their understanding of self and of others and with enhanced insights into what it takes to create and maintain a just and prosperous new globalized world.

This work also rightly draws attention to the tensions that inevitably accompany the interplay of cultures. The news media loves to spin intercultural meeting points as necessarily being conflict-ridden, typically employing phrases such as 'the clash of cultures'. In this way the media ignores the wealth of new perspectives that might readily emerge from fresh engagement with new cultural ways of seeing. Sometimes people say that 'no news is good news' but the media evidently prefers the view that 'good news is no news'. Much more productively, though, Patel, Li and Sooknanan, building upon their own deep intercultural experience, show us how to be open to fresh ways of seeing the world; and this is one of the enormous benefits of an enhanced intercultural communication.

Of special value within this book is its attention to the salience of religion and allied aspects of the sacred as the basis for cultural values and beliefs. In recent generations the West has become increasingly secular, but educators and writers from the West in particular, need to be much more open than formerly to understanding the way in which what is understood as the sacred in many other societies, in fact, underpins culture and then, in turn, informs intercultural communication.

The authors allude to 'the great cultural journey' that they have made in their own experience, which of course has led to this book. Equally true though is that in one way or another, nearly every citizen of this planet is also now undertaking his or her own version of a great cultural journey, as social communication media of numerous emerging kinds, especially mobile phones in developing societies, inexorably infiltrate nearly every society. In previous generations, only the wealthy with time on their hands and an urge to travel could regard themselves as citizens of the world. These days, however, in a sense (like it or not) everyone is starting to attain this status. This book opens the door to the status of a global citizen. In a practical sense, it shows us as readers how to undertake that critical self-reflection which in turn leads us to a better appreciation of and insights into the diversity and cultural wealth possessed by communities worldwide.

Often researchers and commentators rightly talk about the value of indigenous knowledge in societies that are newly encountering the impact of the West, and they describe the importance of honouring such indigenous knowledge. However, the role of true intercultural education, as in this book, should not really be just about putting a barrier fence around indigenous knowledge to protect it as if it is a kind of rare and endangered species. Instead, the larger task of intercultural education is to issue a wake-up call to Western societies and open them (us) to an improved understanding of how the West will benefit from a new understanding, founded on humility and openness, to how we can obtain powerful insights into the historical legacies, practical spirituality, and everyday value systems from which we ourselves might also be enhanced.

## Foreword

You will find argued here the crucial global need for the everyday practice of social justice, along with practice of the critical virtues of patience, tolerance and good faith. These are more than a statement of aspiration: they underpin how we are to relate to others in a global basis, in what is now an essential effort to build a global community in which the dignity of all is valued. As Patel, Li and Sooknanan claim, only when each of us understands how to ground ourselves within our own traditions of family, spirituality and history, can we properly respond and do justice to others whom we encounter in our rapidly-emerging new global environment.

Finally, Patel, Li and Sooknanan offer us their very insightful thought that 'often our voices are one and yet they are unique all at the same time'. Perhaps this is one of the deep and enduring paradoxes at the heart of intercultural communication and one of the special gifts of this book. Each of us needs to be proud of our uniqueness, celebrate our diversity, but, as well, open ourselves to learn from others and then, via intercultural communication, find commonality on how to create a prosperous but sustainable global society. I congratulate the authors of this book for their important contribution to this goal.

Professor Frank Sligo<br>
Massey University, New Zealand

# Preface

Intercultural communication perspectives are relative to one's experience of intercultural communication events and encounters on a day-to-day basis. These perspectives are also fully entwined in our deeply-held beliefs and values that guide our thoughts and actions within and across cultural boundaries. It is, therefore a challenging task to write about intercultural communication in a way that would embrace the deeply-held views from multiple cultures.

Building global communities has for different people a different meaning and for some it might seem an impossible task and a dream. For the authors of this book, the notion of building a global community is a desirable and an achievable goal in the twenty-first century. In fact, it is imperative that we pursue this goal, especially when cultures collide (Lewis, 2006) and continue to collide around us, at perhaps a more intense rate than before as a result of a variety of new communication and transport technologies that have brought more people together at greater speed around the world.

Our own personal histories have contributed to the similar and diverse perspectives on many aspects of global community building and intercultural communication in this book. Our histories continue to impact our present and our future and are significantly bound to our land of birth: South Africa, China and Trinidad and Tobago. However, we have been educated in Western institutions and traditions of thought at some point in our lives and the influence of Western education creates an intercultural conflict within us. Thus, there remains an intercultural tension between our indigenous knowledge, historical legacies, family, spiritual beliefs and value systems, our reality and our Western-educated new identities. Within the context of the book and our writing, it is evident that often our voices are one and yet they are unique all at the same time. We are not a homogenous group even though we may have much in common, but what we aspire to is, building on what we share as the common good. We come from ancestries that have been colonized and which have suffered deep humiliation and atrocities based on race, class, nationality, caste, religion, gender, ethnicity and culture. We lived our lives with the belief that there is good in all people and that there is such a thing as social justice for all human beings. However, 'commitment to a social responsibility ethic is a precondition for social justice' (Patel cited in Naidoo and Patel, 2009). Unless we embrace and implement the social responsibility principles of honesty, integrity, goodwill, fairness, respect and dignity among all people in everything that we do, we cannot justify our claim to uphold social justice. We have to exemplify the belief that all human beings have a right to respect and dignity, to truth and to voice.

Communities across cultures have fundamental beliefs and values that bind their histories and their destinies in a way that seems extraordinary. Philosophies and beliefs across cultural communities manifest their belief in goodness among all people in a variety of ex-pressions that signify compassion, kindness, morality and honour. Examples of these are found everywhere. One example of how these expressions have a common thread is evident in the *Golden Rule* found in the resources and the literature of the Tanenbaum Center for Interreligious Understanding formed in 1992. The *Golden Rule* outlines the fundamental beliefs and values from 12 different religious and cultural perspectives, which all have a message for global understanding that suggests that both mankind and nature must be treated with the same respect that one feels is deserving of one. The 12 religious and cultural perspectives in the *Golden Rule* include Zoroastrianism, Taoism, Sikhism, Native American, Judaism, Jainism, Islam, Hinduism, Confucianism, Christianity, Buddhism and Baha'i. These 12 perspectives are noted at the start of each chapter.

Our intention is to enable every individual to embrace intercultural communication as an open agenda, where all participants in inter-cultural communication events and encounters have equal opportunity and responsibility to make it a positive experience. We hope that this

Preface

experience will become the foundation on which to build a harmonious
global community that embodies mutual cooperation and understanding and one that remains firmly committed to respect and dignity
for all. We hope that the book would be useful in advocating human
rights for all, regardless of their diverse worldviews. Respecting and
understanding diversity means that one recognizes, appreciates and
accepts that individuals and groups approach life from their varying
worldviews and that no specific worldview can be the dominant one.

We believe that the book would inspire corporate and educational
staff, development consultants, human rights officers, employment
equity managers, programme and course designers, teachers and learners,
healthcare professionals, legal practitioners, government policy makers
and politicians to develop and build a sustainable global community.
It is important that each individual and group approaches the promotion
of intercultural communication events and encounters, *only after* they
have undertaken a critical self-reflection of their own stereotypes and
prejudices. Stereotypes and prejudices have become internalized among
us over time and they interfere with our natural human inclination to
accept other people for who they are. Thus, it is the deep introspective
and critical examination of *self* that would be useful in encouraging a
deeper understanding of intercultural concepts and respect for diverse
communities. Only after one revisits one's own fears and anxieties and
challenges one's internalized notions of stereotypes and prejudice within
the consciousness, can one truly embrace the notion of global community
building and support it through the development of intercultural communication skills, strategies, competencies and dialogues within one's
immediate community.

Part I of the book, 'Concepts in Intercultural Communication',
provides a theoretical framework based on communication studies and
mass communication literature, as an attempt to provide a basis to
understand how and why the concept of intercultural communication
becomes complex when critically reviewed in relation to the environment, the expectations and the act of communication itself.

Several perspectives on intercultural communication are offered by
the authors and they bring their own unique perspective to the discussions. Common concepts and terminology are approached in diverse
ways to provide readers with multiple approaches. Challenges and

barriers to intercultural communication emerge in each chapter and they are examined and reviewed positively, so that we can move forward together as a global community that has the courage and the conviction to overcome adversity with renewed faith in humanity.

Part II of the book, 'Critical Perspectives in Intercultural Communication Events', offers the readers real-life everyday events that have either been positive or negative experiences of interactions across cultures around the globe. Each chapter focuses on a different aspect of the deep structure of intercultural communication. We deliberately moved away from the concept of case studies and scenarios because we wanted to present global events as they occur as news media stories. News media stories have been adapted from a range of sources with the intention of providing a real-life event as close as possible to its original form. The selected events represent different realities for the readers and much of their interpretation is embedded within their individual and collective cultural understanding and perceptions of the world around them. These are real life events that happened and that require careful examination of the cultural contexts in which they have occurred. Klyukanov's (2005) principles of intercultural communication, such as positionality and grounding are crucial considerations in how we respond to these events. Questions that may help readers to critically examine each event include:

- How do our stereotypes and prejudices affect our interpretation of an event?
- What are the principles of intercultural communication that operate in the interpretation of the event?
- Which environmental factors influence the response?
- How would the other cultures represented in the event perceive the event?
- How do they interpret the issues in focus?
- What media reporting mode affects the event and why?
- What social responsibility commitments are necessary to avoid such events?
- How do the social justice principles apply in interpreting the events?

\*\*\*

## Preface

It is important to keep in mind that the authors do not offer quick-fix solutions and that they suggest different approaches and considerations in understanding an intercultural communication event. Their perspective is presented as another way of looking at themselves and the world, as they make their way to their respectful places in the global cultural mosaic. Intercultural communication will be viewed more positively when communities around the globe begin to embrace notions of *third culture* and *global community building* as a desirable and acceptable way of life. Only when these notions permeate through a society's cultural fabric, can it be said that all people have successfully contributed to building a global community.

The authors bring into the discussions, their experiences of intercultural communication, knowledge of the field of communication studies and mass communication, and perceptions of intercultural communication as a woman and as men from diverse ethnic, racial and cultural backgrounds. They put forward what they perceive to be the world around them, based on their life struggles and experiences as people who have endured over centuries and decades derogatory labels, indignities and disrespect throughout their ancestry to present day. Through their historical past, their insecure present as residents, immigrants and migrants, and the unknown future of themselves and their children, the authors have worn these offensive labels—as people of colour, kaffirs, minority, non-white, blacks, brown and yellow people, coloured, boat people and people 'fresh of the boat' (FOB), plane people and people 'fresh of the plane' (FOP), coolies, niggers, sand niggers, coons, *Chinee*, goons, *crabrangook*, yellow peril, *Chinaman*, *dougla*, *chamaar*, *kujaat*, *bandaar*, *kirwal* and bound coolie—with a quiet patience, a deep tolerance and with humility, but they have not lost their respect and love for all human beings.

Fay Patel, Mingsheng Li and Prahalad Sooknanan

# Acknowledgements

We acknowledge the wisdom and faith of our parents, our families and especially, our children. Our children encounter intercultural communication events in various forms in their daily lives as a result of the colour of their skin, language, religion, culture, ethnicity, gender, their family names and their historical origins. It is when they are asked by strangers to identify themselves in terms of *who they really are* and *where they really come from* that stereotypical and prejudicial threads begin to weave a web around their persona. It is then that identities, beliefs and values come to emerge as significant characteristics defining their intercultural selves. It is then that our children are forced to confront their cultural and ethnic identities and yet, until that moment, their dignities had remained intact.

Our parents valued education and recognized it as a fundamental characteristic to improve our social conditions and thereby, improve chances of our acceptances into various groups and communities, both dominant and minority ones. Education was perceived to be the key to higher income, better material comforts and a prominent place in society.

We thank all those who have influenced our thoughts and ideas about publishing a book on building global communities and intercultural communication perspectives. Over the years, discussions, meetings and collaborations with our colleagues and acquaintances around the globe have provided endless opportunities to reframe our ideas and to reshape these into a perspective that would encompass the values and beliefs of multiple cultures.

We are indebted to Professor Frank Sligo, Head of School of Communication, Journalism and Marketing at Massey University for honouring us by writing the *Foreword* to our book. Frank's expertise and knowledge in the field of communication studies in New Zealand, and internationally, is especially impressive. His deep insights into various complex issues of intercultural communication, locally and globally, provide a good framework to situate the critical issues of the book.

***

Fay is extremely indebted to her two co-authors, Mingsheng Li and Prahalad Sooknanan, who provided ongoing constructive feedback, support and encouragement. Mingsheng supported Fay with several versions of the earlier proposal since 2006 and especially when her husband took seriously ill. Prahalad was kind enough to join the co-authorship in 2009 and continued to provide additional support when Fay herself suffered a health setback.

Fay is grateful to Katherine Quinsey for introducing her to Canadian multiculturalism within the context of the University of Windsor in Ontario, Canada. She is also appreciative of the rich exchange of perspectives on human rights, equal opportunity, cultural diversity and intercultural communication with Karen Roland and Cheryl Henshaw, with whom she worked closely at the University of Windsor to promote a socially just learning environment. Fay also thanks Gillian Lay (Manager, Professional Development Unit) at Flinders University, Adelaide, Australia for her insights and perspectives on cultural diversity challenges within the institutional context. The many hours of discussion and reflection on various aspects of the cultural diversity project were useful in gaining a deeper understanding of the challenges and issues (e.g., gender, race and class) that remain peculiar to the Australian cultural landscape in this new era.

Fay also dedicates this book to her late parents, Ahmed and Amina Essack Gangat; her brothers Golam Gangat and Yusuf Gangat; and her sisters Bilkis Mohamed Kara, Fawzia Haroon Master and Khairoonisa Yusuf Hatia, who live in Durban, South Africa. She is grateful to them for their love, support and encouragement without which she could not have embarked on this great cultural journey that took them to five countries—South Africa, the United States of America, Canada, New Zealand and Australia—over the past 12 years. In every country, they confronted racial, ethnic, national and cultural challenges but they met every challenge with a special resolve. They found that racism was everywhere and that there is no true democracy in the developing world or in the developed western nations. However, their cultural travels have made them know themselves better through deep critical self-reflection and they have learned through a critical analysis of their own cultural and social mores to understand diverse communities more profoundly. Most important of all, they learned that family, spirituality and history have *everything* to do with who they are, how they view the world around them and how others perceive them.

\*\*\*

Mingsheng is grateful to La Trobe University, Australia, for its scholarships, without which he could not have completed his doctoral study outside China and without which he would not have embarked on his professional journey of intercultural communication and international education. Mingsheng and his family encountered countless cultural challenges, racial issues and institutionalized prejudices manifest in the difficulty they experienced in accessing schools for his daughter's education, finding decent employment and renting suitable accommodation. They were deprived of their Chinese nationality and their Chinese passport became invalid when they became New Zealand citizens. They are deeply aware of cultural issues and the importance as well as challenges of being a global citizen and building global communities.

\*\*\*

Prahalad wishes to acknowledge the assistance of the Organization of the American States for the award of a doctoral fellowship to read for the degree in Communications at the Bowling Green State University. He is particularly grateful to SUNY, College at Potsdam for the opportunity to teach intercultural communication thus reinforcing his interest in the field. The experience of teaching the subject to students on the Akwesasne Mohawk reservation remains the defining moment in his teaching career. Prahalad is particularly grateful to the lead author, Fay Patel, who has offered him the opportunity to share his intercultural experiences in this book.

\*\*\*

We thank our research assistant, Kay Govin (Karpagam Govindaswamy), for her unique viewpoint on various aspects of the manuscript as a Singaporean attempting to settle in Australia. Kay's research assistance (identifying current intercultural communication events, reviewing the references, formatting and preparing the manuscript for submission to SAGE Publications India) was indeed valuable to the authors. Her critical cultural lens provided important insights and yet another cultural perspective on the content. Kay dedicates her contribution to her son Kabilan. Kay would like to thank Dr Fay Patel for giving her the opportunity to be part of this intercultural quest to build a global community.

\*\*\*

We also thank Farhaan Patel for designing the *Diversity Circle* that illustrates the different layers of developing diversity and for his technical assistance with the graphics. Farhaan's personal insights into various aspects of intercultural communication events and encounters were invaluable especially as these were based on his long journey through different lands (in particular, South Africa, United States of America, Canada, New Zealand and Australia) as a child, a youth and now as a young adult.

Undertaking the task of a collaborative book publication is a huge challenge especially when one works across three countries and we are indeed grateful to the technological advances that made it possible to communicate across time and space through the virtual networks. It was the passion and fortitude of all the three co-authors over the past four years and the invaluable assistance from the research assistant which led to overcoming the complex challenges of daily life, family commitments and health, and to reach this final stage of publishing their first book on intercultural communication perspectives. Of course, embarking on an ambitious and creative book project such as this one meant that all contributors had to find inspirational moments to pursue their passion in the private spaces of their lives.

Fay Patel, Mingsheng Li and Prahalad Sooknanan

# Concepts in Intercultural Communication

In Part I of the book, insights are offered into various concepts that have been the pillars of intercultural communication literature over decades. Particularly, concepts are discussed and illustrated from the authors' standpoints and are based on how they came to receive the intercultural messages that were embodied in a range of perspectives. For example, the concepts stereotyping, prejudice and discrimination may have commonalities for the authors on a general level, but their specific experiences and perceptions of these concepts were situated in different cultural contexts. It is their unique experiences as 'people of colour', minorities and non-white people, that make this book stand apart from other perspectives on intercultural communication.

The basic concepts are recognized as important pieces of the cultural mosaic of human life, and how they come together as a whole or not are crucial to the understanding of how they are perceived and experienced. Shapes and colour, for example, are perceived in creative, unique and different ways.

In Chapter 1, the authors suggest that third culture building is an important theoretical framework for building a global community. However, to recognize third culture as a shared and negotiated culture is to go beyond the commonly held notions in intercultural communication literature that has underplayed this concept as a favourable community building perspective. Of course, since most of the intercultural communication literature emerged mostly from West-centric perspectives which come from individualistic societies, it is possible that the collective community building concept was either not favoured or considered as significant. The traditional perspectives that emerged out of Europe, the United States of America, Canada, the United Kingdom, Australia and New Zealand, for example, suggested that intercultural communication is knowing how to behave among other cultures, to accommodate foreign cultures and to get other cultures to adapt and assimilate into the dominant cultures. Traditional perspectives on intercultural communication did not emphasize the importance of analysing your *self* and your *consciousness* and to *know yourself* first, in order that you would know what is valuable to other cultures. The notion of a shared culture based on mutual respect, without subjugation and dominance of participating cultures, does not feature significantly in intercultural communication literature from past decades.

The 10 chapters in this section bring various issues into focus to encourage critical self-reflection. Chapter 1 clarifies and discusses the notion of global community and third culture building, suggesting that there are important considerations in taking such an approach. Chapter 2 offers an overview of the vast fundamental concepts and terminology in the intercultural communication literature. In this chapter, concepts and notions are clarified so that readers can easily follow the discussion and engage in self-critical reflection about their own stereotypes and prejudices as a departure point. Chapter 3 presents a review of the surface and deep structures of culture that affect intercultural communication. While the relationship between surface and deep structures of culture is a well-known fact for many experts and students of communication studies, it is not commonly held knowledge nor does the lay person make an easy association between the two levels of cultural structure. The surface and deep structure of intercultural communication are intrinsically linked, but we frequently engage at the surface structure level, which is on the margins where we judge other culture's values by their form of dress and food preferences, for example. We either ignore or are oblivious of the fact that form of dress and food preference are embedded in the belief and value systems that originate at the deep structure level of family, religion and history of diverse cultures. Chapter 4 introduces the notion of global community engagement, and the consideration of various effective strategies in establishing global community engagement remains a key objective. Chapter 5 critically assesses what it means to be a global citizen. Responsibilities and pressures on individuals who aspire to global citizenry are analysed. Chapter 6 examines the challenges of intercultural communication in the global workplace. Many of these challenges and barriers are familiar to migrants and immigrants who try to find a space between retaining their identities, adapting to a new cultural environment and resisting assimilation for fear of losing their own identity. Chapter 7 concentrates more fully on the influence of environmental and global contexts in intercultural communication. Chapter 8 explores technology as cultural power and the impact it has on intercultural communication, while Chapter 9 reviews critical issues arising across the different chapters and identifies six principles for global community building. Chapter 10 provides a scaffold between the theoretical framework and the practical implications of intercultural communication in a day-to-day, real-life situations. It is also an intermediary chapter that connects the different theoretical concepts and suggests that the practical application of such theoretical frameworks is problematic and challenging when real-life situations occur.

The authors have used the traditional approaches to intercultural communication as a departure point. They suggest .that the older approaches to intercultural communication which focus on learning about other cultures and becoming more competent in identifying cultural differences and 'fixing' communication conflicts by using appropriate cultural norms, are not suitable for a new century in which shared understanding and mutual respect are imperatives. However, the underlying goal of presenting the fundamental concepts in their traditional forms of understanding and use, is to allow readers the opportunity to recognize these concepts as significant influences in the present day. More especially, readers are encouraged to aspire to higher levels of understanding of human interaction across cultures through critical consciousness raising and to move themselves to action in transforming society. The authors encourage critical examination of *self* and *conscience* and urge readers to first know themselves so that they may begin to know others. The emphasis is on understanding one's deep-seated stereotypical, prejudicial and discriminatory behaviours that give rise to fears and anxieties of the unknown and lesser known cultures around us. In this way, individuals and groups can transcend the barriers that surround them and which give them their narrow, myopic views of the world around them.

# Chapter 1

# Building a Global Community

Baha'i: 'And if thine eyes be turned towards justice, choose thou for thy neighbour that which thou choosest for thyself.' *Lawh'i 'Ibn'i 'Dhib, Epistle to the Son of the Wolf*

## Introduction

The increased movement of diverse global populations in the twenty-first century has become more complex than we may have imagined even five years ago. Lee (2003: 3) claims that 'developments in transportation and communication technology have been rapidly removing geographical boundaries' and that people also *move across cultural boundaries*. As migrant populations seek employment, investment opportunities and new geographical spaces to enjoy better security and peaceful coexistence, the goal of building *a global community that can work in harmony* will remain a very significant phase of our lives this century. As global communities come together to live, to learn and to work in all regions of the world where they become active participants in public life, building global community values will remain a challenging task. Global community refers to people of national and international origin who form a community within and outside of a physical space and who subscribe to a diverse range of norms and values that inform their visions and perspectives about the world around them.

The notion of building a global community refers to a willingness by individuals and groups to integrate acceptable cultural norms and values in a meaningful and respectful way into their everyday lives. Implementation of the goal of building global communities within an identified context—corporate organization, educational institution, as well as corporate and community services, for example—encourages a favourable partnership in which social responsibility and account-ability for actions are situated within the framework of the broader participating community that engages in that intercultural com-munication event in any way whatsoever. All societies have in common a deeply ingrained integrity and compassion that allow them to create and to nurture a harmonious relationship. The book explores ways in which global communities may establish a compassionate approach to intercultural communication, so as to build relationships that will encourage the engagement of diverse global communities in meaningful ways. The underlying emphasis in this book is to identify critical perspectives in intercultural communication that help to establish a global community that shares common beliefs and values about what is acceptable and good for all of humanity.

In this chapter, Klyukanov's (2005) 10 principles of intercultural communication are considered as relevant to global community building and the notion of building a global community is analysed and dis-cussed. The concept of third culture building is examined as a viable option, different perspectives are explored and challenges in developing a global community are considered. More importantly, the notion of global community building focuses on common virtues and proposes a reciprocal, harmonious exchange of cultural goods or wealth among participating cultures.

It is important to clarify our own and our combined notions of what is meant by 'building a global community', especially in view of the fact that the globe is shrinking fast. McLuhan's (1962) 'global village' has materialized with intensity and a human complexity that even he may not have imagined. In the twenty-first century, there are more opportunities to travel to more countries at a faster pace and the advancement of the world wide web has heralded a new era of virtual suspension in a space that cannot be underestimated and in a race towards the ultimate dream: a world that is modern, industrialized, well-fed, properly sheltered, safe from war and one that we want our children to inherit as a green, clean mass of future. While we attempt to find our place in this new world that we desire and while we remain suspended in limbo as a virtual global society, it becomes imperative that we begin to clarify our notions of building a global community and to bring this important perspective into the mainstream of intercultural communication discourse.

Klyukanov (2005) advocates 10 principles in intercultural communication and although he does not mention global community and third culture building, the idea of third culture and global community building is implicit throughout his discussion of the 10 principles.

The *punctuation principle* (2005: 21) suggests that mutually acceptable boundary lines must be drawn in order to engage in respectful cultural exchanges and this is a desirable aspect of global community building. The *uncertainty principle* (Ibid.: 43) encourages the reduction of uncertainty through a process of negotiation and sharing of relevant information to eliminate uncertainty. The *performativity principle* (Ibid.: 71) would certainly help participating cultures to cultivate new shared meaning. Cultures that participate in the global community building context need to position or ground themselves within a specific context and to stand their ground; this is known as the *positionality principle* (Ibid.: 99). Third shared culture building can occur by finding common ground in the *commensurability principle* (Ibid.: 126). Klyukanov's (Ibid.: 152) *continuum principle* transcends binary thinking by considering multiple perspectives. The *pendulum principle* (Ibid.: 178) considers the ongoing interaction among cultures to arrive at shared meanings. The next principle highlights the transactional component of global community building and is known as the *transaction principle* (Ibid.: 206). The *synergy principle* (Ibid.: 232) emphasizes the cooperative nature of the relationship among cultures and favours an integration of resources. The *sustainability principle* (Klyukanov, 2005: 258) underlines the primary goal of the notion of global community building which projects a long-term mutually respectful relationship that is built on tolerance, trust and truth.

## Notion of Building a Global Community

Building global communities through a wide range of approaches, strategies and critical self-reflection of one's own stereotypes and prejudice is a massive task when one considers the complexities that surround intercultural communication events and encounters worldwide. However, this book brings a positive message because the authors believe that building global communities is an attainable and honourable goal; one that requires a deep respect, love and compassion for humanity, commitment to social responsibility and upholding of social justice, and the belief that together we can overcome adversity.

It is envisaged that while individuals and groups may have a range of personal and professional roles in their different societies, they also have social responsibility roles. Their social responsibility roles create an imperative for them to make a concerted effort to contribute to global community building. Of course, as mentioned earlier, critical self-reflection of one's own stereotypes and prejudices forms a basis of the global building process. It is only through critical self-reflection and knowing who you are and how *you*—your actions, expectations and assumptions—affect and influence intercultural interaction that you may discover ways in which to build a global community. It is only when we examine our deep-seated beliefs and values and analyse these against the beliefs and values of other global communities that we come to the realization that we have much in common. It is when we recognize and embrace the shared characteristics from each culture that we begin to construct a third culture that is acceptable to our multiple worldviews. Klyunanov's 10 principles of intercultural communication have relevance at different points of the global community building process. For example, the *continuum principle* (Ibid.: 153) would be useful in exploring shared characteristics if one acknowledges that *intercultural communication is a complex space shared by interacting cultures, where meanings exist as different positions along the same continua.*

## Third Culture Building Theory and Perspectives

The notion of building a third culture is not a new phenomenon as it has been researched and cited (Casmir, 1978; Lee, 2003; Fong and Chuang, 2004) across various fields over the past decades. For example, Snow (1959: 70) first used the term 'third culture' when he wrote of the cultural divide between the scientists and literary artists. He wrote that there was a development of a third culture but that it was too early to speak of its existence. However, third culture building is underplayed and under-represented in the area of interpersonal and intercultural exchanges and in intercultural communication events. The authors of the book concur with Lee (2003: 4), who contends that the third culture theory is a useful and 'new perspective from which to look at interpersonal communication in an intercultural setting'. Interpersonal communication across cultures allows cultural exchanges that impact the success or failure of intercultural communication. The notion of third culture building has been alluded to by Klyukanov (2005) in all of the 10 principles of intercultural communication. Each of the 10 principles contributes to different degrees across the vast spectrum of global community building. Lee's (2003: 7) summary of third culture theory is useful in understanding its place in global community building. According to Lee (Ibid.), third culture theory is expansive, responsive, future-oriented and open-ended with growth potential. However, Fong and Chuang (2004: 63) differ slightly from Lee in suggesting that third culture building refers to the outcome of 'the dynamic process of cultural adaptation and intercultural communication competence'. Building a global community is an extension of Fong and Chuang's product-oriented and narrow notion of third culture building and strongly favours Lee's perspective as summarised above. In our view, third culture building within a global community context focuses on engaging goodness and exchanging cultural goods or wealth. It provides open spaces for development, capacity to transcend multiple boundaries, flexibility to be reshaped and accessibility to impending possibilities. Third culture building is framed within the principles of social responsibility, social justice, negotiation, and love for humanity, respect and dignity. This is a noble aspiration in the twenty-first century and many individuals and organizations have demonstrated their commitment to this goal. One example among others is the establishment of the Elders organization in 2007, which was based on the concept of elders in more traditional communities who offered their wisdom and advice in resolving conflicts. Distinct criteria for selection included independence, international trust, demonstrated integrity and inclusive, progressive leadership. The mission of the Elders is to 'support peace building, help address major causes of human suffering and promote the shared interests of humanity' (The Elders, 2007). Prominent global leaders in the organization include Nelson Mandela, Jimmy Carter and Kofi Annan.

Nonetheless, it is possible that when people have little or no under-standing of what third culture building is, they may be sceptical of the notion and may reject it altogether. For some, third culture building may be a threatening concept, if it is interpreted as the loss of one's culture and the giving up of fundamental beliefs and values. For others, building a third culture may be an extension of their fundamental beliefs that align to the reciprocal nature (the 'give and take' principle) of community building and a natural process of evolution of human interaction, and yet for others it may be viewed as embracing the broader human community as a necessary and important aspect of their worldview of all people being 'one family'. Lee (2003: 6) contends that 'in the third culture perspective, cultural domination and subjugation are rejected, but opportunities for mutual development are provided'.

So there are different perspectives on what third culture building is and how it can positively impact global community relations and inter-cultural communication. For example, Casmir (1978: 249) claimed that the third culture perspective 'focuses on the situational and inter-actional communication processes between individuals from various nations and cultures'. This notion was further defined and clarified over the decades by Casmir and Asuncion-Lande (1989: 294), who suggested that third culture building transcended mere conjoining of separate cultures and that it also resulted in 'the product of the harmonization of composite parts into a coherent whole'. This supports our conviction mentioned earlier that building a global community on the foundations of third culture building theory suggests that all communities have the capability to create and nurture a harmonious relationship. Diversity among global communities ranges from ways in which they understand and approach the fundamental needs of human life to ways in which they view gender, age, class, ethnicity, caste, religion, family and history. We realize that life and death, spirituality, family, regional affiliation, truth and evil are aspects of the 'circle of life' that we all revere and understand well from varying perspectives. These perspectives and unique approaches are embedded in the knowledge of indigenous and other cultures; although often indigenous knowledge is not given the respect and recognition that it deserves. We understand that there is no right and wrong approach to life's many challenges but that there are unique and creative approaches that diverse cultures use. Third culture building ensures that we retain and hold steadfast to what is unique to every culture; and yet at the same time also encourages the sharing of common beliefs and values. One important goal of third culture building is the belief that the participating cultures are keen to engage goodness at all times and focus on common virtues.

## Engaging our Goodness and Cultural Virtues

Engaging goodness and cultural virtues in third culture building refers to an emphasis on what is good and virtuous within and across cultures. The sharing and exchange of cultural beliefs and values such as honesty, integrity, respect and dignity are important cornerstones of building a third culture among participating cultures. This suggests a radical shift in interpersonal and intercultural communication literature that has claimed for decades that effective communication across cultures requires intercultural communication competencies, empathising with other cultures, and knowing the customs and habits of different cultures.

Much of the literature in the field (Lustig and Koester, 1996; Eckert, 2006; Suderman, 2007) emphasizes these attributes of successful and desirable intercultural communication as a way to 'know other cultures better' in order that we may engage with them more appropriately. We have subscribed to the intercultural communication competence literature and notions in several chapters as approaches to guide the critical examination of *self* and *the consciousness*, so that people can work on reducing their dependency on stereotyping and prejudices to interpret cultural messages when engaging in intercultural communication events and encounters. The third culture building perspective moves away and beyond the negative and less favourable notions of inter-cultural communication. It begs a shift from the dependency on stereotypes to inform one about communication across cultures and moves one to a higher plane of identifying what is valued and good across the participating cultures.

So global community building on the basis of third culture building as espoused by the authors of this book endorses the belief that critical self-reflection and empathy, for example, are stepping stones to unlearn and de-programme oneself from the social internalization of stereotypes and prejudice that has influenced one's life over several decades. It is a long and painful process to unlearn and de-programme one's stereotypical and prejudiced antenna. However, third culture building transcends the intercultural competency level of intercultural communication that focuses on empathy and 'fitting into the shoes of the other' or being culturally appropriate and accommodating. It moves to a level of dignity for all participating cultures in negotiating a mutual exchange of their culture virtues, thereby promoting and celebrating an exchange of their cultural wealth.

## Exchange of Cultural Wealth

Cultural wealth in this discussion refers to the mutual and respectful exchange of cultural ideas, knowledge, stories, approaches to the culti-vation of food, and so on. It is during the process of exchanging cultural wealth, that participating cultures will focus on mutual cooperation and respect for the cultural wealth of the other. In this way, the established third culture creates a space for welcoming the cultural wealth of par-ticipating cultures. Lee's (2003: 9) research and study of third culture theory among married couples across diverse cultures supported the hypothesis that 'the higher the level of third culture building people experience, the less culture shock they feel'. The hypothesis was operationalized as 'consisting of equality, commonality and transcendence of relationships' (Lee, 2003: 15).

While diverse communities bring goodness, cultural virtues and wealth to the shared third culture, they also face various barriers and challenges.

## Challenges in Developing Global Communities

Among the challenges that one can expect to face in developing global communities are:

1. *Language barriers*: Of course, with English being the dominant language in countries like Australia, Britain and the United States, global communities have to be proficient in English in order to negotiate their socio-economic pathways within that community.
2. *Priorities in cultural values and world views*: Diverse communities may all have several cultural values in common. However, the priorities that they place on cultural values may affect their worldviews. This in turn will impact the negotiability factor in building the global community culture.
3. *International politics*: International politics and the political economy of the globe will ultimately interfere with which communities are willing to engage on what level. Natural resources, political power, the hegemonic imbalances of the world's larger and smaller nations, the poor and the rich nations, are all factors that determine which global communities will continue to embrace goodness. Different levels of social and economic development would lead to a situation that continues to replicate the traditional dominant model of international development from the early twentieth century where some cultures remain in a subjugated role while other cultures maintain their dominance.

4. Difficulties to achieve a global 'one size fits all' community culture
   The notion of a 'one size fits all' global culture is not a feasible one and the global community model will have to remain diverse and creative so that it will continue to embody a richness of culture and a love for humanity that comes in different shapes and sizes.

## Conclusion

Third culture theory building, the fundamental foundation for building a global community, goes beyond the older and more familiar theoretical frameworks in intercultural communication that have a repertoire of condescending language where other cultures are 'accommodated, assimilated, adapted and acculturated'. Lee (2003: 17) contends that third culture moves away from the reductionist ethnocentric view that one culture is subjugate to or dominant over another culture.

In Lee's (Ibid.: 8) view, 'third culture is negotiated and harmonized in an area' in which individuals 'can communicate beyond their original culture'. We believe that the time has come for intercultural communication to subscribe more seriously to the third culture building theory as a way to move towards a future where diverse cultural communities will no longer be subjugated or be dominated by more powerful cultures, regardless of their control over the political economy of the globe. Third culture building will ensure that global communities come together on the basis of respect and dignity.

Chapter 2

# Overview of Intercultural Communication

Buddhism: 'Hurt not others in ways you yourself would find hurtful.'
*Udana-Varga, 5:18*

## Introduction

Intercultural communication is a complex concept that has taken on a wide variety of meanings and interpretations. According to Klyukanov (2005: 45), intercultural communication is a 'process that is inherently variable and subject to interpretation'. While individuals and groups bring their unique and special meanings to this term, in the most basic sense, intercultural communication means that some form of culture and some form of communication has interacted or intersected in a particular space, time and context.

However, it is at the point of intersection that a range of complex issues arise. It is important to note that this complexity results from the intricate link between culture and communication. At the point of intersection, questions are posed such as:

- What is being said?
- Why is it said?

- Who is saying it?
- Where is the communication taking place?
- When is it taking place?
- What meaning is conveyed?
- Why is it said in that way?
- How is the message being interpreted?

In answering these questions, it is essential to note that what a person says suddenly becomes immersed with who the person is and the focus shifts from the content (what is being communicated or said) to the cultural identity of the individual (who is saying this and how it is being said, negotiated and interpreted). In other words, the social customs of that culture become the area of focus than the actual information in the communication. It is this interweaving of one's cultural identity with forms of communication that creates the complexity in the interpretation of the message that is delivered.

This chapter provides an overview of the fundamental principles in intercultural communication. It identifies its key concepts, discusses how these concepts contribute to a positive or negative interpretation of intercultural events and critically addresses issues related to perception, stereotypes, prejudice and ethnocentrism. The chapter provides a framework for understanding how and why we interpret and react to intercultural communication events in the way we do. It also encourages us to self-reflect on our own worldviews and that of others in a way that we may begin to see the world differently. Particularly, it engages us in a discourse that requires our combined efforts at effective global communication and building global communities on the basis of mutual respect and understanding.

## Defining Intercultural Communication

There are many definitions of intercultural communication by experts who offer different interpretations and meanings. The definition by Samovar and Porter (2004) emphasizes that a person's perception of the world around him/her is deeply entrenched in the system of symbols that his or her culture uses to make sense of the world. Further, they claim that intercultural communication is the 'interaction between people whose cultural perceptions and symbol systems are distinct enough to alter the communication event' (Samovar and Porter, 2004: 15). The importance of understanding cultural perceptions and symbol systems will be discussed in detail later in this chapter and will continue to emerge as a theme throughout the book. However, in spite of the numerous definitions, it is important to note that during an intercultural communication event, problems arise as a result of a person:

1. not recognizing the uniqueness of the individual,
2. not focusing on the message,
3. not understanding the belief systems and values upon which cultures are established, and
4. making judgements from the perspective of one's own culture.

In other words, people—individuals and groups—contribute to the problems through their interpretations, or rather their misinterpretations, of the intercultural communication event.

People are the key complex component in all communication within and across cultures because they communicate their cultures along with the message. People, therefore, are the human factor that affects intercultural communication.

## Understanding Communication and Culture

Communication is a dynamic and constantly changing process that is part of a larger context. One does not communicate anything to anyone without that communication being affected by a multitude of factors. Therefore, the interpretation of the messages sent and those received is not a simple and straightforward process. Interpretations are open to any number of interventions or interferences along the way and these include everything from the cultural symbols associated with the individual or group to the context of that communication. Individuals and groups are always inferring meaning through a connection of the 'dots' or symbols. Inference is a critical skill in attempting to understand and make sense of an intercultural communication event; however, it can also lead to making wrong assumptions.

Whatever the nature of the communication, it allows for self-reflection as we examine our set of assumptions about the communication event; often though we ignore the fact that every communication event has a consequence. However, as mentioned earlier, communication is complex because people are both similar and different in a number of ways.

Among the characteristics that make people from different cultures similar and different are their cultural beliefs, values and their social norms or customs. Through communication and socialization, people may share certain common cultural characteristics but they may differ on other aspects. The similarities and differences are usually attributed to the beliefs and values embedded in such things as their history, tradition, education, religion and family structure. All of these beliefs and values are learned and passed down to different generations through a range of communication processes such as mass media, language, education, stories, folktales, mythology and proverbs. Learning one's own culture is called *enculturation* and it may be learned either directly or indirectly.

## Connecting Culture and Communication

Culture is complex in nature because it is constantly changing. For instance, migrant populations need to adapt to new ideas and values in the dominant culture they move into, and while they will keep most of the features of the existing culture, they will also borrow a range of others from the new culture. This adaptation to new or dominant cultures is referred to as *acculturation*. Also, cultures are integrated systems because they do not operate in a vacuum. In other words, cultures are deeply entrenched in, affected by, connected to, and dependent on other parts and processes of a system.

The foundation or pillars of cultural systems are the beliefs upon which their values rest. Values are a set of system rules that guide the culture and usually are often non-negotiable. The values of a culture are also prioritized—a hierarchy of beliefs and values is established and members of that culture are expected to conform to these cultural priorities. Beamer and Varner (2008: 8) claim that 'cultures rank what is important. In other words, cultures teach values and priorities'. These values and belief systems create the conditions upon which cultures form their reality of the physical and social world around them.

Individuals and groups in a culture perceive the world from their own cultural beliefs and value perspectives. A culture's perspective or worldview often determines how members of that culture interpret the communication events around them. This is why individuals and groups from different cultures are accustomed to making judgements on the actions of other cultures based on their own belief and value systems. According to Samovar and Porter (2004: 46), 'culture affects perception and communication'. Culture, therefore, is a significant factor in how people communicate and how they perceive any form of communication.

In order to understand a culture, one has to understand its belief systems and values, and how that culture makes sense of its environment. It is only when you understand how a culture perceives the world around it that you will be able to communicate effectively with people from that culture.

# The Relationship between Context and Communication

Communication does not take place in a vacuum. Communication at all levels, from individual, organizational, national to international, takes place in a particular context. Contexts play a very important role in interpersonal, intercultural and international communication. Context consists of five aspects—physical, social, psychological, temporal and physiological:

1. *Physical:* location, environment, distance, setting, infrastructure, noise, temperature, seating arrangement and technology.
2. *Social:* power, hierarchy, rules, norms, formality, history, relationship and gender.
3. *Psychological:* attitudes, feelings, emotion, perceptions, tones, pressure, stress, trauma, self-concept, views, feelings, bias, stereotypes, prejudice and prior experience.

4. *Temporal*: time and timing.
5. *Physiological*: health, well-being, illness, disability and hearing loss.

The study by Knapp and Hall (2006) suggests that physical contexts can greatly affect our communication behaviour. The learning environment—lighting, room temperature, arrangement of furniture, interior decoration, structural design, colour, sound effects, object mobility, distance and size of the classroom—can influence students' communication behaviour and learning outcomes. They noted that 'more intimate communication is associated with informal, unconstrained, private, familiar, close, and warm environment' (Ibid.: 107) and less relaxed and more superficial and stylized communication is associated with greater formality. Further, they pointed out that social environment often shapes one's behaviour. A violent and poverty-stricken social environment often 'encourages or fosters unconventional and deviant behaviour, or at least tolerates it' (Ibid.: 110).

Contextual factors affect our perception and the way we encode and decode a message. The same message may carry different meanings in different situations. What is appropriate in one situation may not be appropriate in another. For example, our communication styles differ greatly at home, at the workplace and at a national or an international conference. Talking to a friend in a bar is different from talking to a foreign dignitary on formal occasions. In many Western countries, political leaders are used to criticisms from the media and individual citizens. When such a communication pattern is transferred to other social contexts, individuals may experience serious culture-related problems. In Thailand, individuals showing any sign of disrespect towards the royal family may face years of imprisonment. Disrespect towards and insults of the royal family in Thailand are legally forbidden. In August 2008, Australian writer Harry Nicholaides was arrested and put into Thai prison for insulting the royal family in one of his novels written three years before, relating to rumours about a Thai uncrowned prince's love affairs. He was released in February 2009 after the royal pardon.

Contexts provide clues to interpreting and understanding the underlying causes of a particular event. It should be acknowledged that people living in a socio-cultural environment must comply with rules and norms of that society. These norms and rules frame the communicative behaviour of the group. Failing to comply with these cultural rules and norms can bring about punishment and sanctions. Take adultery, for instance, all cultures prohibit it; however, attitudes towards adultery differ from culture to culture. While it is a ground for divorce, it is not a crime in Western Europe, North America, Australia and New Zealand; however, it is given the death penalty in some Islamic countries. Therefore, intercultural communication requires a good knowledge of the specific context and contextually appropriate communication behaviour.

Another aspect of contextual influence—time and timing—also has an enormous impact on communication. An unnecessarily lengthy meeting may create a boring environment. Failing to meet an appointment may communicate a message of the person being unreliable, untrustworthy and unable to perform an assigned task. Lecturers who cannot finish lectures on time can annoy the students and get low rating in their feedback. Timing is critically important to get your message across. For example, if one has a great idea that one wants to communicate to the manager, it may lead to a frown one day and a smile on another. This is because people are more receptive at some times of the day compared to other times. It is necessary to assess the state of people's emotion, mood, time schedule and the time of the day. For instance, it is certainly not a good time to discuss an important idea with the manager at mid-day when it is lunch time for most people or at 5 or 6 o'clock in the afternoon when everybody else is rushing home and when the manager has already been exhausted and does not have enough patience.

The physiological context involves an individual's real or perceived physical and mental health, disorder, well-being, disability and stress. All cultures possess specific beliefs and views about illness and health, which have been passed down from generation to generation (Samovar, Porter and McDaniel, 2010). Individuals' cultural and ethnic backgrounds can shape their perceptions of their well-being, physiological conditions and illness in both the physical and spiritual realm. For example, when a Tibetan has a toothache, he/she may not visit a doctor and instead visit a shaman, a person acting as a medium between the visible and spirit worlds. The shaman spits into her mouth in an attempt to reduce or cure her pain. When unwell, some people may think they are obsessed by demons. To them, ridding the patient of the evil spirits requires exorcism. In 2007, for instance, Janet Moses, a 22-year-old mother of two, died in Wellington, New Zealand, during a ceremony performed by more than 30 *whanau* members. She was drowned as water was forced into her eyes, nose and throat to flush out the demons. This has caused a huge debate about religious and cultural practice and legality. In the end, it was seen as a religious and cultural mistake and the five Māori were exempted from imprisonment for the exorcism killing of the woman.

# Factors that Affect Intercultural Communication

When we communicate with people from other cultures, we may not recognize the many factors that affect our communication. As we have seen, the most influential factor in nearly all intercultural communication experiences is the human one: people and the beliefs and values of their own cultures.

A major contributing factor to our behaviour in an intercultural communication event is the *mass media*. Media in the form of television, radio, newspaper, songs, music and the Internet, all play an important role in helping us to form our own opinions, make judgements and influence our perceptions and therefore our communication with individuals and groups of people.

Intercultural communication is also influenced by the quality of the *intercultural contact* that we have in our personal and professional environments. Intercultural contacts have increased significantly in recent years around the globe because of better, faster and easier access to transport and information technologies, and by an increase in migration caused by ethnic conflicts, environmental factors and the attraction of a better lifestyle in a more stable economy in another part of the world.

Language barriers can also be considered as a factor. Language is a medium for communicating cultural values and beliefs. Even when people assume that they can speak each other's language, chances of miscommunication are very high. Erroneous inferences may be made purely because of one's partial understanding of the message sent. Even when people can speak another language fluently, selecting the appropriate words as well as the non-verbal elements of communication such as body language, gestures, clothing, pitch, intonation, concepts of time and space can consciously or unconsciously affect our communication. For example, face-covering Islamic clothing, popularly described as the *niqab* (covers the face leaving only the eyes visible) and the *burqa* or *hijab* (covers the head leaving the face uncovered) have become a controversial political issue in Western Europe, New Zealand and in Australia (see Photographs 2.1 and 2.2). Some intellectuals and political groups advocate prohibition for various reasons.

Making assumptions about the other party and misinterpreting each other's motives can be another factor affecting intercultural communication. For example, in a riot that broke out in Lhasa, capital of Tibet on 14 March 2008, it was agreed among a majority of Chinese nationals that the Tibetan rioters committed violence, murder, arson and other acts of savagery against civilians, and caused huge damage to public and private property, and the riot was considered to be 'an outburst of hooliganism and wanton violence' (Jacobs, 2008). Therefore, they supported the Chinese government's response over the riots. Many Western leaders and the Western media, however, expressed their sympathy for pro-Tibetan agitators and urged the Chinese government to stop the arrests and immediately release the rioters. The unrest was described by the Western media as 'a revolt against the oppressive rule' (Ibid.). Several Western leaders seized the opportunity and demanded that China open dialogues with the Dalai Lama who had been advocating Tibet's 'maximum autonomy' and the 'Greater Tibet'. The Chinese government, on the other hand, interpreted his demand as independence. The riot was therefore considered as a manipulative move by the Dalai Lama and his followers as a flashpoint to put international pressure on China's policy over Tibet. China regarded Western involvement in the Tibet issues as a blatant interference with its national sovereignty and integrity. The tension between China and some Western countries sparked waves of protests and demonstrations involving pro-Tibet activists and pro-China supporter during the Olympic torch relay in 2008.

**PHOTOGRAPH 2.1:** Woman wearing a *niqab*

**PHOTOGRAPH 2.2:** Woman wearing a *burqa* or *hijab*

These are only a few of the many factors that affect intercultural communication in some way. Other factors such as stereotyping, prejudice, ethnocentrism and perception can also have a huge impact on communication. It is important to remember that all cultures have features that are both similar and different and because of this fact intercultural communication events can be altered positively and negatively at any given time.

# Cultural Features

If we accept that every culture has features that are both unique to that culture and also common to other cultures, then we need to examine those features to understand why people in different cultures behave the way they do. An examination of cultural features will help us understand why some people may live in harmony with their environment while others will always be at odds with their environment.

Establishing typologies of a range of cultural features and the behavioural patterns of cultures have been the subject of investigation over the past decades by various researchers around the world. It is now commonplace to quote those research outcomes to review those typologies and to access those classifications to explain intercultural communication phenomena. However, if we keep in mind one of the most remarkable features of a culture is that it is constantly changing, then some of the research outcomes may not hold true for the same culture as an entity and may not be generalized over time. Since cultures change over time and the variables are constantly changing, the outcomes may not even hold true for all members of the same culture. The only features that we may accept as true or long-standing are that cultures are:

1. Organized according to a hierarchy of cultural priorities,
2. have both distinct and common patterns of behaviour and they are recognized most often by their unique qualities,
3. established on a set of beliefs and values,
4. interrelated and interconnected,
5. influenced by a wide range of factors,
6. dynamic and subject to change but the core cultural values often resist change,
7. symbols for people to communicate the meanings of the practices (see discussion in the next section), and
8. are a stabilizing mechanism for the society.

Culture is not an inborn attribute. It is a learned human quality, 'a social inheritance' (Charon, 1999: 94) transmitted from generation to generation through various ways, such as schools, media, stories, art, families and oral traditions. Communication through language makes culture a continuous process in which cultural values, beliefs, norms of behaviour, principles, attitudes and moral standards are formulated and transmitted. In this enculturation process, we learn by listening, watching, reading, imitating, observing, experimenting and internalizing and practising the rules and norms embedded in the culture. A ceaseless process of learning helps form our thinking habits, behavioural patterns and mental programming (Hofstede, 1991) in response to other people's actions, events, social tasks and environment. Finally, enculturation enables us to become a member of that society.

Culture influences our communication behaviour; communication can also influence culture. Each can affect the other. Thus, cultural values are the products of sociality and communication. Through interaction, a social group or community creates *theories* to explain the experience of reality. These *theories* become a *template* or rules of socially expected norms of communication behaviour. In turn, these rules become institutionalized and made into tradition to become important parts of social reality (Littlejohn, 1992). Individuals and groups participate in the creation of their perceived reality. However, people from different cultures and societies construct and perceive *reality* differently because of differences in their upbringing, education, and political and social contexts. As people perceive and interpret *reality* from their own cultural perspectives, problems in intercultural communication are highly likely to occur. What is good and acceptable in one culture may be bad and unacceptable in another culture.

## Cultures as Symbols

All cultures are based on symbols which help a culture to create, maintain, formulate and transmit its thoughts, traditions, customs, values, beliefs and norms to its members or members of other societies. We all communicate in symbols, which have shared and mutually understood meanings. It is difficult to imagine how miserable our life might be without symbols to help us learn, live and communicate with others.

There are a wide range of manifestations of symbols, the most important one being language. Language shapes the reality in which culture lives, influences people's thinking processes, thought patterns and behaviour, and helps its members find their proper place in their own culture or in this world through language codes. It is a powerful tool for us to communicate our ideas, values and beliefs. For example, American President George W. Bush coined the terms 'rogue states' and 'axis of evil' in the late 1990s to refer to North Korea, Pakistan, Iraq, Iran, Afghanistan and Libya, countries that he felt might threaten the national security of the United States. Linguist Noam Chomsky (2000) considers such terms as being a justification for American imperialism, as well as a propaganda ploy by the Bush administration.

Other manifestations of symbols can be various and diverse, not only verbal but also non-verbal such as artefacts, buildings, handicrafts, carvings, manners, gestures, colours and numbers. Different cultures use different symbols to express their ideas. When communicating with people from other cultures, it is important to understand the codes of these symbols. For example, each piece of Māori greenstone carvings is full of meanings. A fish hook suggests good health, strength, determination and smooth sailing. A single twist, for example in a shape similar to the number 8 represents the joining of two individuals for eternity, trust and loyalty. A double or triple twist stands for the bond between two individuals, the connection, interdependence, friendship and relationship with people from other cultures or societies. The twist shape indicates that there may be ups and downs in our life, but we will remain bonded and our joint effort can help us overcome our difficulties.

Some Chinese from the southern part of China have superstitious beliefs in numbers. They do not like the number 4 because the sound is close to die. However, they have a passion for the number 8. The sound is close to Cantonese *fa*, which means wealth, prosperity and good luck. Some would spend millions of dollars purchasing a car plate or a phone number with more than four 8s.

The implication of the preceding discussion is that intercultural communication has the potential to build a global community. We therefore need to understand the cultural symbols underpinning cultural values, beliefs, assumptions and norms of behaviour patterns.

Knowing the surface meanings of the symbols is not enough; we also need to explore the deep meanings so as to have a more rounded picture of the cultural.

## Surface Culture and Deep Culture

As we have mentioned in the previous discussion, culture is presented in many forms, some tangible and some intangible. We use *surface culture*, also called *objective culture*, to describe the tangible aspects of culture, such as people, buildings, artefacts, art, dances, music, songs, food, dress, language, behaviour, actions and gestures. The iceberg resembles a culture where the tip of the iceberg floating above the water represents the surface culture which is about 10 per cent, while 90 per cent of the mass of the iceberg is hidden below the surface and thus invisible, representing the deep culture (see Figure 2.1).

**FIGURE 2.1:** Iceberg illustration of surface and deep culture

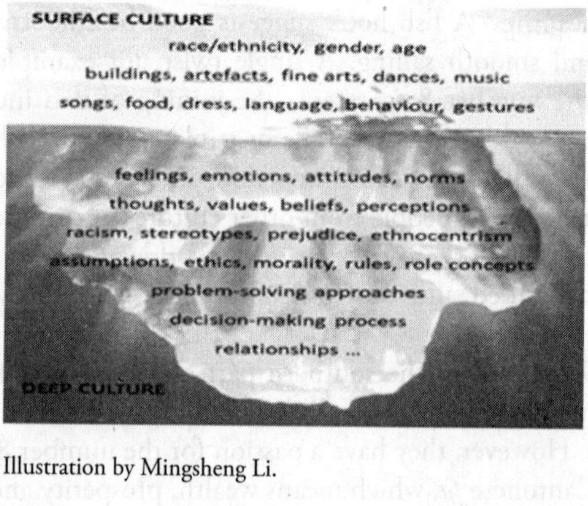

SURFACE CULTURE
race/ethnicity, gender, age
buildings, artefacts, fine arts, dances, music
songs, food, dress, language, behaviour, gestures

feelings, emotions, attitudes, norms
thoughts, values, beliefs, perceptions
racism, stereotypes, prejudice, ethnocentrism
assumptions, ethics, morality, rules, role concepts
problem-solving approaches
decision-making process
relationships ...

DEEP CULTURE

Illustration by Mingsheng Li.

*The deep culture*, also called *subjective culture*, refers to the intangible aspects of culture, such as feelings, emotions, values and attitudes. The deep culture is hidden and difficult to see at the surface level and yet it is what primarily determines how the people behave and communicate with each other, and how we interpret our experiences.

Nevertheless, there is no absolute dividing line between surface and deep cultures. They are interrelated and inseparable. The surface culture also reflects the unconscious frameworks of meaning, values, norms and hidden assumptions. For example, a building may be an expression of the values and beliefs of a particular culture. The Māori Haka is performed for a number of reasons: for amusement, as a welcome to distinguished guests, or to acknowledge great achievements or occasions (McLean, 1996: 46–47). Māori cultural values, beliefs, history, mythology and attitudes are reflected in the Haka.

Cultural differences at the deep level are more difficult to perceive. To understand deep culture, we need to interact and communicate with people of that culture and experience it to learn the culture. Books, movies and mass media can be very useful ways to understand a culture, but they can also reinforce stereotypes. For many new migrants, understanding the deep culture of the host society can take a long time. Cultural adaptation is in fact cultural learning. It can be a neverending learning process. Lack of sufficient knowledge of the deep culture of the host society can generate negative feelings and experience among temporary sojourners. For example, Asian international students are the international group who are the least satisfied with their learning and social experience in New Zealand (Ward and Masgoret, 2004).

# Stereotype

Walter Lippman (1922) borrowed the metaphor *stereotype* from the printing lexicon, which originally means a duplicate impression and a fixed and unchanging process of an original typographical element or image whenever it was applied. He described stereotype as 'pictures in our heads' (Ibid.: 16). Whitley and Kite (2006: 6) define *stereotype* 'as beliefs and opinions about the characteristics, attitudes and behaviours of members of various groups'. Thus, a stereotype is a standardized mental picture held in common by individuals of a social group based on oversimplified opinions and incorrect and uncritical judgements. Our memory and our experiences in a particular context such as the influences of mass media, schools, families and peers, play an important role in forming such stereotypic mental pictures. Stereotypes can never be completely accurate because they are often based on some kernel of truth that has become simplified and generalized due to such factors as racism, ethnocentrism, historical events, imagination or fabrication.

Stereotypes represent a shortcut in collecting, processing and interpreting information about a cultural group by perceiving people according to their social categories rather than their individual characteristics. The shortcut is used as a handy tool to help us reduce our memory load by making inference and prediction about the group without having to perceive it first-hand.

The effects of stereotypes can have positive and negative effects. Positive stereotypes may promote the image and reputation of the target group while negative stereotypes may lead to justification of ill-founded prejudice, ignorance and self-fulfilling prophecy for the stereotyped group, and preventing these people from succeeding in the society. The September 11 attacks, for instance, on the twin towers in New York City by alleged terrorists have activated negative stereotypes, especially by media, among the general public against Arabs and Muslims. Government policies, customs checks and immigration policies single them out. These negative stereotypes lead to suspicion, fear and hate and they continue to act as filters even to this day.

## Prejudice and Discrimination

Very often the differences between the two terms—stereotypes and prejudice—are not clear. Stereotypes are used as a shortcut to make a generalization of the characteristics of a social group whereas prejudice expresses unfavourable attitude toward a social group and its members. The latter emphasizes unfair, irrational and adverse feelings based on preconceived judgements, and an attitude of hostility directed against an individual or a group without any grounds. Prejudice therefore involves 'the affect or emotion one person feels when thinking about or interacting with members of other groups' (Whitley and Kite, 2006: 7).

The reasons for prejudice can vary from person to person and group to group. Prejudice may be derived from one's emotional reactions to a social group. One's negative experience with a particular member of that group may foster the belief that all members of the group are alike. Media, education and perception also play an important role in forming people's attitudes and opinions.

Prejudice is associated with discrimination. Discrimination makes a distinction in favour of or against an individual or a group based on stereotypes of the group, class and categories. The dark side or negative part of discrimination is prejudice. 'Prejudice and discrimination' before 'can create communication barriers leading to racism'. Perceptions and stereotypes are regarded as truth and reality, and may exist in schools, hospitals, workplaces and in international relationships.

Prejudice and discrimination are subtle in nature and are not easily discernable. For instance, the unemployment rate in a country can be a reliable indicator of reality. According to a report by the New Zealand Department of Labour (2009), the annual average unemployment rate for 2008 was highest for the people from the Middle East, Latin America and Africa (11.8 per cent each), followed by Māori (9.2 per cent), Pacific peoples (7.8 per cent), European/Māori (6.7 per cent), Asian (5.5 per cent). The lowest unemployment rate was for Europeans (3.1 per cent). This government report shows that people from the Middle East, Africa and Latin America are most discriminated against in employment.

A UMR public opinion survey in New Zealand found that 74 per cent of respondents felt that Asian people experienced prejudice and discrimination in the country. One out of five reported having been personally discriminated in the past year, all being related to race and ethnicity (New Zealand Human Rights Commission, 2009).

Sometimes, a single event can change people's attitudes toward the members of the group and thus develop prejudices. After the massacre at the Virginia Polytechnic University in the US on 16 April 2007, it was found that the killer, Cho Seung Hui, was a South Korean. The negative attitude and anger of Americans began to emerge towards Asian students and Asian communities, particularly Korean students and communities in the US and in other parts of the world. To mitigate the negative impact of the backlash and the mounting anger, South Korean President, Roh Moo-Hyun expressed his shock, sorrow, and a collective sense of regret and guilt over the shooting, even though they did not regard the killer, an American citizen, as a typical Korean (Veal, 2007).

Racial prejudice and discrimination are two of the biggest obstacles in intercultural and international communication. Although all human beings belong to the same species, *Homo sapiens*, races are distinguished by their body shape, skin, eye and hair colour. We have more common traits than differences. Racial prejudice or ethnophobia—any irrational fear and hatred of any race or ethnicity different to one's own—is characterized by intolerance and discrimination, and can result in apartheid and segregation. As a social disease, it is deeply rooted in the minds of some cultural members and it affects everyone. History has recorded countless examples of atrocities and tragedies through ethnophobia: Afro-American slaves working on plantations; Hitler's killing of six million Jews; the poll tax levied on the Chinese immigrants in New Zealand, Australia and Canada; ethnic cleansings in Bosnia, Iraq, Ethiopia and Somalia. Other extreme forms of acting out racial prejudice and ethnophobia include honour killings. On 4 April 2007, Du'a Khalil Aswad, a 17-year-old Kurdish girl of Yezidi religion in Iraq was stoned to death for having had a relationship with a Sunni Muslim boy in a nearby town. She was condemned to death as an honour killing by her relatives because her relationship with a boy from another religion was believed to have brought shame to herself, her family, relatives and the tribe. It was believed that an honour killing could redeem the family honour.

Prejudice is considered an unacceptable human behaviour in many liberal democratic societies. It can lead to racial discrimination and a violation of human rights. In New Zealand, for instance, the Human Rights Act 1993 is implemented 'to advocate and promote respect for, and an understanding and appreciation of, human rights in New Zealand society'. The victims of prejudice may be denied access to those resources that are necessary for people to thrive and succeed such as access to employment, education, health care and housing (Vaugham and Hogg, 1995). Prejudices by nature, even in their implicit form, can be unshakeable even in the face of evidence to the contrary. They distort our perceptions and prevent us from assuming a correct stance and taking appropriate actions.

## Ethnocentrism

Ethnocentrism is another barrier in intercultural communication. It is a mindset that perceives the values, beliefs, tradition, language, history, religion, behaviour and ethnic standing of one's own social or cultural group as being superior to all others. An ethnocentric person tends to judge other social and cultural practices and behaviour from the perspective of her own standards. Ethnocentrism is based on assumptions and over-generalizations without any substantial evidence about other people and other cultures. It impedes effective communication with other social and cultural groups and exaggerates the importance of one's own culture while denigrating the values of the others.

The real challenge in intercultural communication comes from hidden ethnocentrism, which is not publicly articulated and is difficult to detect. It exists in one's mind; yet, it is rarely challenged. Everyone is ethnocentric to some degree even though most people believe they are rather open-minded, tolerant and mindful of cultural issues. It is reasonable to assume that our own group or culture is superior to others because the process of enculturation through education, history and socialization has programmed our mindsets in such a way that we are often unaware of the 'blind spots'. In the field of scientific research, for example, Teo and Febbraro (2003) argue that there exists 'scientific racism' which sees certain human groups as inferior to Europeans and Americans.

Kam and Kinder (2007: 320) maintain that ethnocentrism has become a bedrock in the American mindsets 'that powerfully underwrites support for the war on terrorism' that is 'undertaken against a strange and shadowy enemy'. While waging the war on terrorism, the United States, with a strong conviction of their ethnic superiority, imposes

American cultural values in the forms of freedom, democracy and human rights on countries they have conquered or are going to conquer. To their surprise, the war on terrorism begets more terrorism. Living conditions are now far worse for most people in Iraq than they were before 'liberation' from Saddam Hussain. Few Iraqis appreciate their 'liberators'. American cultural values have not successfully colonized the minds of the people they have liberated.

Ethnocentrism often takes a binary view: We are superior and you are inferior. Those deemed inferior are often blamed for something that has gone wrong in society. In New Zealand, for example, immigrants are often identified as the causes of many social problems such as the rising housing prices, issues with health care, street crimes and unemployment. As a result, cultural diversity cannot be seen as an asset but as a threat to the society. It is seen that whenever there is an election, immigrants from Asia, the Middle East and the Pacific Islands are bound to become the target of political manoeuvre and manipulation. Thus, ethnocentrism in such manifestations can be a divisive force in a multicultural society.

## Perceptions

Underlying most intercultural communication problems are perception problems that arise from a mismatch and differences in the frame of reference. Stacks, Hill and Hickson (1991: 4) point out that 'communication brings us together and perceptions tend to separate us'.

Perception is the process of acquiring, organizing and interpreting any sensory information. It is shaped by our prior experiences, cultural values, beliefs and socialization, and can influence our reception of knowledge, the way we think and behave, and the impression we form of others. The goal of effective intercultural communication, therefore, is to negotiate and create shared meaning by understanding each other's perceptions.

We interpret and assign meanings to other people's verbal and non-verbal behaviour based on our knowledge and past experience—our mental categories or representations. Gregory (1998: 3) asserts that 'an amazing 90 per cent or more of an interpretation depends on past knowledge stored in the brain'. The closer the behaviour is to our mental data bank built on past knowledge and experience, the more likely it makes sense to us. On the other hand, incongruence or mismatch can lead to misunderstanding and irrelevance.

As perception is based on our experience, it is selective and subjective. Reality is, but shared perception. If we share similar experiences, it is easy for us to understand each other. One object can give rise to many interpretations if we do not have common experiences. If one has never experienced anything through his/her senses, it is difficult to process new information when you cannot find a match from your memory data bank. For example, if you have never seen or heard of *koala*, you do not know what it is because you cannot find it from your memory bank. But when you see a photo of this Australian animal that feeds on the leaves of the eucalyptus tree, you get to know what it is by processing and interpreting this sensory information. Next time when we talk about *koala*, we may find some common background and common experience.

# Intercultural Communication and Global Community

Globalization has shrunk the world. This is especially true due to the impact of new communication technologies such as the Internet. The world today is therefore globally integrated, interrelated and interdependent. A global cultural flow in social, technical, cultural, political and ecological spheres has changed the international landscape and the way we communicate. It has had an enormous impact upon our intercultural understanding and behaviour.

In Appadurai's (1990) view, cultural flow includes five dimensions: ethnoscape, mediascape, technoscape, finanscape and ideoscape. Appadurai coined these words with the suffix *-scape* from *landscape* to refer to 'the historical, linguistic and political situatedness of different sorts of actors' (Ibid.: 296) navigating all the perspectives that these landscapes can offer. These dimensions—migration, media, technology, finance and ideology—have combined to promote a new world in which we, as global citizens, share concerns over global issues and expect to make joint efforts to address issues such as poverty, health, environment, climate change, avian flu, terrorism, sea-piracy, human and drug trafficking. Tackling these issues requires a global mindset and cooperation in decision-making and problem-solving. Most important of all, they require us to become aware of all the areas of intercultural communication if we choose to be global citizens. New information and communication technology, as well as fast and effective transport systems, connect us to people around the world. In this way, we become exposed to various opportunities to integrate both local and global perspectives in intercultural communication and to share our concerns as a global community. Building a global community through shared concerns means that we have to understand and respect a broad range of cultural value and belief systems.

The increased movement of diverse global populations, goods and ideas in the twenty-first century has become more complex than we may have imagined even five years ago. As migrant populations seek employment, education, investment opportunities and new geographical spaces to enjoy better security and a peaceful coexistence, the socio-political goal of building of global communities will remain a very significant phase of our lives. A *global community* refers to people of national and international origin who form a community within and outside of a physical space and who subscribe to a diverse range of norms and values that inform their visions and perspectives.

The notion of global community building recognizes that no intercultural communication endeavours can be complete unless we recognize the global influences on an intercultural communication event as presented through various sources. As global communities come together to live, to learn and to work in new and old regions of the world where they have become active participants in public life, building global community values will remain a challenging task. However, such a challenge enhances our transformative learning. The learning process in cultural encounters allows individuals to assume flexible identities, to navigate the unchartered social and cultural terrains without following rigid rules of fixed group identities, and to embrace communication, locally and globally, with people from diverse backgrounds.

## Conclusion

Culture shapes our communication behaviour and communication in turn shapes culture. They are mutually inclusive and interrelated. Intercultural communication is therefore anchored on the interface or conjuncture of culture and communication. Therefore, it is important to understand the basic theories and concepts of both culture and communication. Communication and culture are both extremely complex because we are both similar and different. We are similar because as human beings, we share certain universal values and beliefs. People in one culture share most of the values and beliefs of that culture. However, people from other cultures do not have much in common in their cultural values and assumptions.

Cultural disparities arise from differences in values, perceptions, norms and expectations. These cultural differences may cause communication barriers when we receive, process and interpret the message being sent. Many factors can affect our interpretation and negotiation of the meaning, such as an individual's cultural knowledge, language and communication skills, experience and contexts. Some traits such as stereotypes, prejudice and ethnocentrism can blind our eyes and prevent us from successful intercultural communication. To communicate effectively with people from other groups or cultures, not only do we need to be aware of the dark side of these traits, but we also need to take proactive actions to avoid them or to reduce their negative impact.

Cultures are presented at both surface and deep levels. Just like the two sides of a coin, they coexist. The deep culture requires the surface presentation and the surface culture is a manifestation of the meanings of the deep culture. Understanding the deep culture, however, requires efforts and constant learning.

All cultures use symbols to communicate with the members of their cultures or other cultures. The meanings of symbols can be learned, shared and transmitted. The most important cultural symbol is language. Symbols that are deemed important to one culture may not make any sense to other cultures. Understanding symbolic representations of a culture, verbal or nor-verbal or graphic, helps us to understand the deep root of that culture.

Intercultural communication involves interaction with people from different cultural backgrounds. The cultural flow in the form of migration, media, finance, technology and ideology has quickened the pace of globalization. The process of globalization is therefore forcing us as global citizens to rethink our intercultural communication strategies to bridge cultural differences and address our common concerns by building a global community.

# Chapter 3

# Exploring Surface and Deep Levels
# of Intercultural Communication

Christianity: 'In everything do to others as you would have them do to you; for this is the law and the prophets.' *Matthew, 7.12*

## Introduction

Intercultural communication is defined and interpreted in different ways. Klyukanov (2005) claims that intercultural communication is a process that is inherently variable and subject to interpretation, and this is a significant underlying belief from which we can analyse events of intercultural communication. Samovar and Porter (2004: 15) perceive intercultural communication as 'interaction between people whose cultural perceptions and symbol systems are distinct enough to alter the communication event' which brings the aspect of complexity into every intercultural communication media. Fong's (Fong and Chuang, 2004: 13) definition of intercultural communication emphasizes the 'culturally different communication styles where differing patterns of communication exist' and this is usually the first point of departure in intercultural communication discussions. Discussions begin and end with the different communication styles, placing emphasis on 'differences' without synthesizing the salient aspects of how different communication styles may contribute to a common or deep or significant understanding of an intercultural communication event. Whatever definition we subscribe to, we have to recognize and understand that intercultural communication operates, both at surface and deep levels. More importantly, it is the deep level that helps us to understand how people from different cultures communicate.

This chapter examines in greater depth the concepts of surface and deep levels of intercultural communication. The discussion aims to demonstrate that it is only through a critical reflection on the variables affecting intercultural communication at either level, that we can begin to build our global community on firm pillars of respect and dignity for all. It is important to raise awareness and understanding on how the surface and deep levels of intercultural communication affect and influence our intercultural behaviour in the public sphere and also lead to multiple ways of interpreting intercultural events.

## Surface and Deep Levels

The interpersonal level of intercultural communication usually occurs at the surface level of intercultural communication and is often the primary subject and discussion point in a wide range of literature on intercultural communication (Eckert, 2006; Hall, 2005; Gudykunst, 2005; Lustig and Koester, 2006). For instance, in many organizations, the focus on interpersonal relationships is usually based on a superficial exchange of customs like celebrating cultural festivals by sharing food and recipes. O' Hair, Friedrich and Dixon (2008: 76) are of the opinion that while it is helpful to have knowledge of customs, one also needs to have more information about people 'to anticipate responses and issues that are important' to them. Although the surface and deep levels of intercultural communication are intrinsically linked, many organizations function at the surface level and judge cultural behaviour through forms of dress, food preference and gestures. In this way, cultural stereotyping is used, for instance, to inform the manager about a person's ability, interest and potential. Miller (2003: 250) cites the example of a manager believing that 'Japanese American workers are unassertive or that Mexican American workers are lazy' and suggests that this is prejudice and if the manager uses this knowledge to treat them differently then that amounts to discrimination. Organizations often function at the surface level of interpersonal relationships based on cultural stereotyping, but Miller (2003) claims that engaging in 'sophisticated stereotyping' or 'helpful stereotyping' is not a desirable way to learn more about other cultures and it 'can be dangerous, because it is often incomplete and misleading'.

During interpersonal engagement in an office environment, staff may enquire about religious and cultural norms of minority staff as an information gathering exercise and this could be interpreted as a compassionate and genuine interest in the minority culture. This is a form of socio-cultural engagement on a surface or superficial level. Deep levels of communication may not be explored in the workplace environment because that examination might lead to an interrogation of one's belief and value systems. And yet, unless we examine our own deep roots of culture that shape our beliefs and values, we cannot begin to make sense of the world around us.

Unless we recognize, understand, accept and integrate the various aspects of the deep structures of culture on all forms of communication in an organization, the organization cannot hope to arrive at any significant level of intercultural competence to manage the complex intercultural communication challenges of this century. Organizations must become more inclusive at a deep level of intercultural communication so that organizational value systems are in tandem with employee value systems. According to Driskell and Brenton (2005: 12), 'an organizational culture involves unique ways of doing things in an organization that are best captured by such elements of the culture as the history, norms, and values of a group'. Inclusive organizational environments begin with an appreciation and respect for cultural diversity at the deep root of culture.

Concepts that relate to intercultural communication, such as mental models, stereotypes, prejudice, cultural identity and worldview, deep structures of culture—religion, family, history—and intercultural competence will be reviewed and clarified in the context of this discussion. 'Mental models' is a term coined by Kenneth Craik in the 1940s as cited and endorsed by Eckert (2006: 28). Eckert claims that 'mental models shape what we see, hear, feel and do' (2006: 39). Mental models are sometimes established on the basis of inaccurate information, mixed messages from the mass media and from our social networks. Often, fleeting references to our mental models may lead to miscommunication in an intercultural interaction.

## Mental Models, Stereotypes and Prejudice

When we are confronted with people from diverse cultures, we immediately activate our mental models and begin our mental processing of stereotypes. Mental models allow people to reference stereotypes that have been stored in their subconscious. Eckert (Ibid.) suggests that we use mental models to confirm our biases and use them as 'ladders of inference'. She further suggests that the 'ladders of inference' are based on the stereotypes that we embrace and these stereotypes are pervasive and powerful examples of mental models in our society. Since stereotypes are often based on outward appearance, meaning is generated on the basis of visible data alone. Visible data do not only include skin colour but may also include non-verbal communication such as posture, gesture and paralanguage or how you say something, for example, your accent. We use our stored information together with the visible data selectively but at a rapid pace. Almost in the blink of an eye, we use stereotypical descriptions and make judgements based on our mental models.

It is therefore essential to examine our deeply held stereotypes and prejudices and find ways in which to reduce and remove them. Hall (2005: 203) contends that we use our reference list of 'stereotypes to control our prejudice' and that 'stereotype is a practice' while 'prejudice is an attitude'. More importantly, he claims that we have the power to rid ourselves of prejudice even though we may not be able to eliminate the stereotype. If we fail to recognize and change our prejudiced behaviour, we may become perpetrators of an injustice and have to take responsibility for that. For example, prejudice may be enacted in different forms such as institutional racism and if we are party to a decision of institutional racism, we become accountable and responsible for that decision and the consequences. It is the deep roots and structures of our cultures that shape our worldviews and give us our cultural identity.

## Cultural Identity and Worldview

Cooper, Calloway-Thomas and Simonds (2007: 72) hold the view that 'cultural identity serves as an interpretive devise. It helps us see ourselves along such dimensions as race, ethnicity, kinship, soil, region, gender, and religion'. Gudykunst (2005: 66) supports this view claiming, 'our cultural identities are our social identities that focus on our membership in cultures'. Cultural identity is important to an individual. Samovar and Porter (2004: 84) claim that while we may have a wide range of identities, it is the identities 'gained through deep structure institutions' that matter most. In other words, our cultural identity is infused with our religious, historical and family loyalties and perspectives.

Samovar and Porter (Ibid.) identify three important deep-rooted structures that shape our worldview, namely religion, family and history. These structures, not only shape our worldviews and help us to form our identities, but also influence our perceptions. Making meaning of the world around us, according to Samovar and Porter (Ibid.: 45) is part of the process of perception 'whereby people convert the physical energy of the world outside of them into meaningful internal experiences'. Furthermore, they claim that perception is learned through culture and is used selectively in the form of beliefs and values. Beliefs are deeply embedded and remain unquestioned. They also claim 'cultural values define what is worthwhile to die for...' (Ibid.: 49). Deep structures define the cultural values that drive individuals and groups to choose death as a way to show their deep love for family, religion and country, and provide justification for defending their worldviews. One's worldview may even justify why people choose to kill or die for a cause to which they subscribe. If one begins to examine one's belief and value systems that forms the basis of one's cultural perspectives, it becomes abundantly clear that one might be willing to kill and die for one's country, one's family honour and one's spirituality. In the end, if we examine the deep level of intercultural communication events, and 'position' and 'ground' our viewpoint within the value and belief systems that we subscribe to, we might find a common theme emerging on the values and beliefs that we hold dear to ourselves. For example, our belief in sanctity of life and/or the certainty of death might weave a common thread in how we view the loss of life and the occasion of birth and we use these beliefs that shape our worldviews to interpret and judge events around us.

Our worldviews or perceptions frame our intercultural interactions. According to Klyukanov (2005: 2), one of the fundamental principles of intercultural communication, namely the *positionality principle* states that 'intercultural communication is a process whereby people from different cultures engage in interaction and claim authority for their vision of the world'. Furthermore, he claims that the *positionality principle* refers to 'the cultural knowledge located in a specific context, worldview, and cultural space' and that 'cultural meanings are generated and grounded' (Ibid.: 92). In other words, we make meaning of an intercultural event from our own perspective in an ethnocentric way and we 'stand our ground'. Hall (2005: 31) claims that our 'worldviews operate at an unconscious level' and this means that our worldviews and 'cultural gaze' (Klyukanov, 2005: 89) are stored and utilized without conscious thought. Our worldviews influence how we perceive intercultural events and we tend to use degrees of ethnocentrism which according to Hall (2005: 199) and Klyukanov (2005: 99) ay include positive and negative judgements about how and why other cultural groups react in the way that they do.

In some cases, individuals and groups react emotionally and this may or may not lead to more violent actions. In the latter half of the twentieth century, the media reported a diverse range of worldviews representing ethnocentric perspectives that resulted in either violent or non-violent reactions around the world. For instance, Pope Benedict cited a fourteenth century Byzantine emperor who equated 'Islam with violence' causing deep felt resentment among the world's Muslim population; Chavez (2006) called Bush 'the devil' and won the admiration of the non-western world, while at the same time falling further out of favour with the USA and her allies; an MP in New Zealand said that 'women with *burqa*s and the gay community' were problematic in New Zealand society and in the twenty-first century there are increasing media reports of this trend in Europe and the UK. In the UK, for example, there is a move to ban *hijab*s and *niqba*s from the public schools. Other examples of similar incidents are: the publication of cartoons of the Holy Prophet Muhammad in the Western press; Iran's retaliation to the Muslim cartoon publication was a print cartoons ridiculing Judaism; the French soccer star Zinedine Zidane's head butting incident (World Cup 2006) with Marco Materazzi because Materazzi made an indecent remark about his mother and sister. Materazzi acknowledged that he had insulted Zidane. Zidane said that his headbutting action was 'unforgivable, but they must also punish the true guilty party, and the guilty party is the one who provokes'. Often, the actions of the guilty parties in many intercultural communication events are condoned or they receive a soft rebuke. So one must pause to question why? Is it because of where the power of the justice system lies? Is it because the media reports are biased? Is it because the minority voice remains a distant whisper in the wind? Examples throughout history attest to the complexity of intercultural communication in a global space and especially the prejudices and biases that are exercised in the interpretation of such incidents. It has been noted that up until the present day, anti-Semitic remarks anger the Jews and there is a protected boundary around public references to the Jews and the Holocaust. However, other offensive labels are often less protected in the public space. For example, the derogatory label *negro* and *nigger* that is offensive to African American, African and Arabic speaking communities who have a history associated with it; the label *coolie* that is offensive to South Asian, South African and Chinese communities is also less protected.

According to Klyukanov's (2005: 90) classification of ethnocentrism, some of these remarks result in 'ethnocentric reduction' when we 'reduce other cultures to a shadow of self' and 'ethnocentric negation' when we 'ignore, disregard, and negate other cultures'. While we may be inclined towards judging intercultural events from an ethnocentric perspective, we should subject our judgements to careful scrutiny. Critical reflection from a deep structure level of intercultural communication may help us to understand why people get emotionally charged and why they may be willing to give up their lives and take other lives when religion, family honour and country become the targets of ridicule, insult and persecution.

## Religion as Deep Structure

Worldviews also contribute to the way in which cultures perceive humanity and suffering. According to Scupin (2000: 14), 'a religious worldview helps humans comprehend the meaning of pain and suffering, or evil in the world'. Religion, according to Samovar and Porter (2004), provides an insight into the practices of a culture. Often, mass media and social networks focus on the differences among the various religions of the world. However, they urge us to consider similarities among religions and to address commonality among world religions such as 'sacred scriptures, authority, rituals, ethics, and sacred time'. Cooper, Calloway-Thomas and Simonds (2007: 79) state 'culture and religion are intricately linked' and added to this is our personal identity. In any intercultural interaction, one has to keep in mind that a person's religion is part of his self and hence one should approach a person with deep respect for his religion and his self. Nearly most cultures have experienced either direct and brutal or subtle and covert forms of ridicule, insult and persecution at one time or another throughout history till the present day: from the time of the Roman Empire to the Protestant and Catholic conflicts in Ireland in the twentieth century to the religious wars in Bosnia, Palestine, Afghanistan, Iraq, India and Pakistan, the list is endless. Apart from religion, family is another institution that demands respect and a central place among cultures.

## Family as Deep Structure

Samovar and Porter (2004) claim that family transmits not only culture but also identity. This means that family not only helps you define social skills, gender roles, clarifies the place of age and respect for age in context, but also shapes who you are. Many cultures have deeply entrenched beliefs and values about family. Similar family values are imbibed by diverse cultures. Suderman (2007: 79) agrees that 'the value placed on family is often a major point of comparison across cultures', particularly in collective cultures. Suderman (Ibid.) cites the Chinese, South Asian, Asian, Latin American, Mediterranean, European and African cultures as examples of cultures in which family survival, harmony and honour is extremely important.

It is important to recognize these deep family bonds among many world cultures and to note that maintaining family honour, for instance, may drive family members to kill or to be killed. In other words, sacrificing a life for family honour may not be ruled out as an option. As Suderman (Ibid.) reminds us, strict adherence and compliance with religious and cultural practices might urge family members to take extreme measures to defend family honour. For example, in Medieval Europe, women had to protect their virginity and chastity through chastity belt compliance, which was important to Christian cultural practice. In Muslim cultures, 'virginity among unmarried women' is a basis of family honour. In addition to family, another institution that contributes significantly to cultural identity and that provides a firm grounding principle is history, which includes a person's regional, national or territorial membership.

## History as Deep Structure

According to Cooper, Calloway-Thomas and Simonds (2007: 78), 'identity and territory are associated in human's minds and, by extension, the two influence intercultural communication'. One's historical connections and territorial space is of paramount importance to one's cultural identity. History explains and describes the main features of a culture. It provides specific details and events that shape an individual's identity. What makes you who you are and what shapes your role in a society is the result of where your place was in history and is today. The events you experienced and the actions you will take to reclaim that history will contribute to and shape that history that your children will call their own. As a result, it is necessary to critically assess our histories and to ask who writes the history books, how history is distorted and why some histories are imposed while other histories are obliterated.

On the whole, religion, family and history influence and affect communication among cultures. However, in terms of cultural influences on context, it is interesting to note Samovar and Porter's (2004) view that the greatest recognition of deep structure influence is found in the area of health. Religion and family structures affect and influence individuals and groups in the area of health more directly and more deeply especially in terms of treatment, prevention and non-prevention of ailments. Educational institutions and business organizations do recognize the influence of religion and family on cultural communities, but to a lesser extent. Nonetheless, the influence of deep structures of culture on education and business remain marginalized and ignored. However, intercultural competence or the ability to competently manage intercultural communication events requires an understanding and appreciation of deep levels of culture. Intercultural competence is posited in much of the intercultural communication literature as an option in managing cross-cultural encounters and events.

## Intercultural Competence

Samovar, Porter and McDaniel (2007: 314) claim that 'being a competent communicator in an intercultural encounter means that you have the ability to analyse the situation and select the appropriate mode of behaviour'. Chuang (Fong and Chuang, 2004) also identifies appropriateness and effectiveness as important aspects of intercultural competence. According to Klyukanov (2005), to be interculturally competent, one has to manage an intercultural event across three levels. However, it is important to note that intercultural competency models help to manage the external aspects of intercultural communication events and encounters. Intercultural competency models do not help to interrogate the mental models and internal cultural conflicts within individuals that feed on stereotypical impulses and which lead to prejudiced and discriminatory behaviours. These models do not encourage individuals and groups to critically reflect on the deeply held beliefs and value systems that shape their own worldviews. Critical self-reflection would assist in knowing oneself better and in understanding why others are willing to defend their beliefs and values to death.

Klyukanov (2005: 5) identifies three important components of intercultural communication competence: cognitive (thought/knowledge);

affective (emotional/attitude) and behavioural (action). To be interculturally competent and to ensure the appropriate and effective management of any intercultural communication encounter, all three components will have to be adequately satisfied. Many of the problems in intercultural communication arise out of inadequate and inaccurate information and ignorance about diverse cultures. We continue to mingle with similar groups because it is natural to feel insecure and uncertain in unfamiliar situations and substitute our limited knowledge for the *truth*. Further, we use ethnocentrism to judge other cultures and continue to judge them through our cultural lens while focusing on differences alone. Aspiring toward intercultural competency is, therefore, the first step toward developing appropriate behaviour to effectively manage an intercultural event.

In order to become interculturally competent, intercultural communication scholars (Samovar, Porter and McDaniel, 2007; Hall, 2005; Eckert, 2006) recommend that we develop the ability to manage and respond appropriately to a challenging intercultural situation. Cultures must respect the similarities among them by beginning at the deep structure level. In order to become competent, we need to expand our knowledge of diverse cultures, change our attitudes and display more inclusive behaviour. Most important of all, we have to know ourselves and the only way to do this is to self-reflect and get in touch with our own perceptions and behaviour. Leigh (1998: 33) claims that 'awareness of self as a cultural being is most important in cross-cultural work' and 'the achievement of self-awareness is an ongoing process, never finished'. In addition, one needs to develop empathy or the willingness to imagine the other's experience. When we imagine the other's experience, we do not replace it, we do not delete their experience and we will never have the same experience. Among the effective strategies to be used in an intercultural situation, it is necessary to include communicating empathy, avoid ethnocentric responses, develop communication flexibility, apply the intercultural ethic of seeking similarity, respect difference, seek forgiveness, offer an apology, and finally take responsibility for our actions. Cooper, Calloway-Thomas and Simonds (2007: 300) claim, 'the emphasis on empathic communication is guided by a belief that there is enough common to all of us to warrant human understanding'.

# Conclusion

Samovar and Porter (2004: 23) claim that 'successful intercultural communication appreciates similarities and accepts differences'. Are we ready to shift our focus from differences to similarities and from negative to more favourable notions of cross-cultural encounters that enhance intercultural communication and view it as an enriching experience? Building strong cultural communities globally, based on an understanding and respect for the deep institutions of culture that are the fundamental pillars of intercultural communication, requires commitment from all participating cultures. Dominance and subjugation of cultures cannot be part of that relationship among cultures. Cooper, Calloway-Thomas and Simonds (2007: 87) contend that 'in the twenty-first century we must search for a way out of the limiting and confining aspects of cultural identity'. This should become our goal in building global communities that can flourish within creative and open spaces in which they will build new shared and negotiated identities based on mutual respect.

This chapter focused on the deep roots of culture in order to encourage critical reflection on personal behaviour and actions in intercultural communication current events. In encouraging ourselves to critically analyse our own belief and value systems, it is hoped that cultural communities would begin to understand why other human beings, like themselves, are influenced by family, religion and history. Samovar and Porter (2004: 83) claim that if one had to list cultural values in a hierarchy, then 'at the top of every culture's list would be love for family, God (whatever form that might take), and country'.

# Chapter 4

# Global Community Engagement

Confucianism: 'Do not unto others what you do not want them to do to you.' *Analects, 15.13*

## Introduction

In order for us to function effectively in today's rapidly changing global environment, it is essential to cultivate a range of competencies that are amenable to different intercultural contexts. These competencies would enable us to participate and engage meaningfully with members of the wider global community. This ability is known as *global community engagement* which is dependent on established norms or conventions that assure all individuals and groups the rights to attributes such as mutual respect, social justice, freedom of expression, sanctity of historical and cultural knowledge and spaces, shared dignity and an esteemed wisdom. Empathy and benevolence are other key attributes of engagement in a global community context, especially if individuals display an open and compassionate attitude that fosters goodness in each of us as global citizens.

In this chapter, we propose the following desirable norms of engagement for effective and mutually rewarding intercultural interactions in a global community context: strive for intercultural competence, know oneself, exercise the will to change, re-examine discrimination and prejudice, engage in diversity development and define diversity boundaries. These discussions offer strategies that will assist individuals and groups to assess their levels of readiness to engage others in a global community. Once it has been ascertained where one stands within the established and desirable norms of engagement, it is easier to assess if one is adequately equipped to engage meaningfully with the global community.

## Strive for Intercultural Competence

Eckert (2006) claims that intercultural competence includes refinement of a person's skills, knowledge and attitude. An individual must, therefore, seek to develop an in-depth knowledge and awareness of his/her own culture in order to be effective in an intercultural relationship. This revelation dispels the perception that individuals have to become more culturally aware of the cultural norms and customs of others to become interculturally competent. On the contrary, however, it seems evident that it is more important to first learn about one's own behaviours, cultural quirks, values and beliefs to engage successfully in any intercultural communication event.

Assessing a person's intercultural competence through the required attributes is regarded as a prerequisite for global engagement. Among the desirable attributes, the need to be interculturally competent is uppermost in the minds of experts (Klyukanov, 2005; Eckert, 2006). Intercultural competence requires in-depth knowledge of oneself, conflict resolution skills and optimism in one's outlook. For instance, in order to prepare individuals and groups to study, work and live in a global community environment, organizations conduct a diverse range of orientation and induction programmes in intercultural communication to foster an awareness and appreciation for cultural diversity.

Cultural diversity programmes and initiatives in organizations are built on the notion that it is becoming increasingly imperative to know more about the cultures of others in order to do business with them, to teach in their context and to help them learn in our context. In this regard, it is even more important to know one's own culture to engage meaningfully with other cultures. In other words, one has to look inward on a regular basis to establish why and how one's values and beliefs, stereotypes and mental models, prejudices, cultural norms, communication styles, and verbal and non-verbal behaviour together with other external environmental factors, contribute favourably or unfavourably to the intercultural communication event. Another important component of intercultural competence is the ability to resolve conflict effectively; equally important is the need to cultivate a positive attitude towards cultural diversity.

In adapting Eckert's (2006: 2) intercultural competence pre-assessment for the global context, the following statements become critical in formulating a self-profile of one's intercultural competency levels and diversity development:

1. I am aware of the demographic changes taking place around me and understand the implications for me, my community and the workplace.
2. I am aware of the challenges and associated benefits of cultural diversity.
3. I am always aware of the stereotypes that shape my interactions with others.
4. I do not draw negative conclusions when others do or see things differently.
5. I know what culture is and how it influences my particular values and the unique way in which I view and interpret the world.
6. I have spent time exploring the many facets of my culture and how it differs from others.
7. I recognize that although someone may look very different from me, it is possible that we share lots in common.
8. I am aware that because cultures are complex and multifaceted, I can never assume anything about others.
9. I always strive to get beyond obvious differences such as ethnicity, race and gender, so that I might build effective intercultural relationships.
10. I make a point to learn about other cultures.

11. When I meet someone from another ethnic group or country, I demonstrate an interest in understanding his/her culture.
12. I understand my role in facilitating effective intercultural interactions.
13. I am confident in my abilities to recognize and resolve inter-cultural conflict.
14. I recognize that building the skills necessary to engage in intercultural relationships is an ongoing process.

One's level of intercultural competence can be assessed by agreeing or disagreeing with each of the above statements (1 = not at all, 2 = somewhat and 3 = very much so). If respondents chose 1 and 2 more frequently, then it is more likely that they will need to build their intercultural competency level to a level that demonstrates that they have developed the knowledge, skills and attitude within their personal profiles to engage effectively in a global context. Respondents may want to retake the intercultural competency assessment test after having critically reflected upon the range of desirable norms of engagement in this chapter or after reading the book. They may also attempt the assessment after a period of time that is reasonable in developing knowledge of diversity. As a whole, however, we recommend a pre- and post-test to give the reader a fair indication of his/her diversity development profile.

## Know Yourself

It is essential to *know yourself* before engaging in an intercultural encounter. This knowledge ensures that the encounter is meaningful and beneficial to the parties involved. In this regard, a model that encourages one to self-reflect on his/her values and beliefs is the Dimensions of Diversity Wheel. The Dimensions of Diversity Wheel developed by Loden (1996a) is a useful tool in guiding self-reflective practice to *know yourself* since it provides the primary and secondary dimensions of diversity that form a basis for the self-reflective exercise. An illustration of the Dimensions of the Diversity Wheel can be found online (Loden, 1996b). Diversity issues influence our value and belief systems and contribute to the complexities that we encounter in the public sphere. In every intercultural communication encounter and event, we must first understand what beliefs and values we hold dear in order to respond appropriately to the other. Loden's (1996a) dimensions of the diversity wheel illustrate that the primary dimensions cannot be changed upon reflection, however, the secondary dimensions of diversity can be changed after deep reflective practice. Among the primary dimensions (inner circle) of the diversity wheel are age, ethnicity, gender, physical and mental attributes, sexual orientation and race. These diversity dimensions also define who we are on the exterior in relation to our physical appearance and many of these dimensions are a product of socialization in our respective social spaces. According to Loden (1996a), the secondary dimensions of diversity (outer circle) relate to the less visible attributes of who we are such as geographic location, education, work experience, organizational role and level, and religion among a wide range of diversity dimensions. At this level, we can exercise a fair degree of choice about who we want to be and how we want to be perceived by others with whom we engage in the wider global community.

The primary dimensions emphasize the point that one has little or no choice in determining who they are and/or who they become in relation to their ethnicity, race and age, among others. These elements are visible and definitive so that while one may be described as a 50-plus brown female, another may be described as a 40-plus Caucasian male for example. Primary dimensions also influence our assumptions and affect our mental models on a regular basis, both consciously and subconsciously. They socialize us into our worlds and continue to define who we are and how we perceive the world. For example, the co-authors of this book view the world differently from their Caucasian or Western counterparts. The co-authors' experiences of race, gender, ethnicity, age, physical and mental attributes and sexual orientation also differ from each other based on their experiences of socialization from their own environments, their history, spirituality and family values.

According to Giroux (1999, 2001) and Shaheen (2001a,b; 2006) popular culture gravely impacts our socialization into our primary dimensions of diversity and suggests that media plays a critical role socialization. Giroux and Shaheen's critical media studies question how and why the Disney Corporation for instance, sends powerful messages to children through children's films and cartoons. Their research in this area illustrates our socialization into our roles is often subtle and covert. It also demonstrates that there are multiple factors that contribute to our socialization. Jack Shaheen's (2001a) critical discussion on the negative messages that are relayed by Disney media about Arabs and Arab culture in the Mickey Mouse Monopoly documentary is a point to be noted. Shaheen's book (2001b) and film documentary (2006) on *Reel Bad Arabs* provides further evidence that a powerful media can deliver a powerful negative message to an innocent, young and vulnerable public. According to Shaheen (2001b) Hollywood has depicted today's Arab in the same way that the Arab was depicted in previous years. 'He is what he has always been—the cultural "other"' (2001b: 2). According to Shaheen, in a telephone interview with the Montreal Mirror (2007b), 'Unlike some other stereotypes, there are political implications involved in Arab stereotypes. There is the Arab–Israeli conflict and the demonization of religion. The closest parallel is the vilification of Jews.' Shaheen (2006) and Giroux's (1999) argument that the media shape who we are and how we perceive the world around us is another important aspect to consider when we engage in the global community context. However, not everyone agrees with the notion that media has a powerful and total effect on a passive audience. In the same way, the notion of a passive audience that was strongly advocated in the early 1950s and 1960s by Schramm is also refuted as new communication technologies demand a more active and interactive audience. Today, media is seen as having limited effects on an otherwise active audience, which empowers audience members with the will to change and adapt even in the arena of intercultural communication.

## Be Willing to Change

In terms of achieving the desired level of intercultural competence, we have a choice in changing some dimensions of our visible attributes as well as to exercise control over certain aspects of our fate. We can become who we want to be against all adversity but it must be in line with our will to move above and beyond the visible and invisible barriers around us. Nelson Mandela, for example, demonstrated an incredible will to change his circumstance through his enduring 27 years in prison. One of the inspirational poems that influenced his will to conquer his jailors was *Invictus* written in 1875 by William Ernest Henley. *Invictus* is Latin for 'unconquered'.

### Invictus

*Out of the night that covers me,*
*Black as the Pit from pole to pole,*
*I thank whatever gods may be*
*For my unconquerable soul.*

*In the fell clutch of circumstance*
*I have not winced nor cried aloud.*
*Under the bludgeonings of chance*
*My head is bloody, but unbowed.*

*Beyond this place of wrath and tears*
*Looms but the Horror of the shade,*
*And yet the menace of the years*
*Finds, and shall find, me unafraid.*

*It matters not how strait the gate,*
*How charged with punishments the scroll.*
*I am the master of my fate:*
*I am the captain of my soul.*

Like Nelson Mandela, exercising the will to change means more than just being willing to change. More importantly, it means that you came to engage in the global community sphere not only with a desire to change but that you are aware of your responsibility to make a change if and when the opportunity presents itself. The difference between willing to change and taking an action to change is that one is making a conscious effort to alter one's own behaviour for the benefit of effective engagement within a global community framework. Your commitment to engagement in a global community context becomes visible through your action of changing your behaviour.

## Contemplate Forgiveness and Reconciliation

Another important consideration in building a global community is that people must also be willing to forgive. Forgiveness is one of the most difficult qualities of reconciliation to attain and to show in a conflict situation. However, it is also one of the most honourable qualities to uphold in any situation. Throughout history, when cultural communities have been torn and devastated by war and conflict, there are few communities that contemplate forgiveness and reconciliation. Significant examples from history in which forgiveness was regarded as an important step in reconciling differences include Rwanda, Bosnia, Herzogovina and South Africa. In each case, there was a unique approach to seeking forgiveness and reconciliation and it was dependent on the cultural context of those involved and the nature of conflict.

Reconciliation and forgiveness is extremely difficult when you have been the perpetrator. According to reconciliation educator John Rutayisire (2004), who was a survivor and a perpetrator of the Rwandan genocide, 'the perpetrator needs to acknowledge that he has done something wrong before…the next step of asking for forgiveness…'. It is equally difficult to admit that one has done something wrong which is usually the first step to recognizing that one has had a role in creating the conflict situation and a responsibility in correcting that situation. More especially, as we have claimed earlier, the only way that one can know about how to behave toward others is to first critically reflect inwardly to know oneself. As Rutayisire (Ibid.) claims, '…forgiveness implies a deep level of personal analysis'.

Another important perspective on the willingness to change and to forgive is put forward by Larisa Kasumagic (2004)—a psycho-social support worker for war-traumatized families in Bosnia and Herzegovina— who speaks about the principle of healing before reconciliation. In her view, healing comes before reconciliation and most importantly, Larisa focuses 'on healing yourself [by] facing yourself' as a recommended strategy towards reconciliation. She regards healing of the inner self and soul as 'inevitable for the whole process of reconciliation' (Ibid.). Healing was also an important part of the South African approach to reconciliation.

The South African truth and reconciliation process in the post-Apartheid years was a unique alternate approach. According to Dullah Omar (1997), 'the issue of amnesty was essential to the sort of truth-telling and justice-serving that South Africa needed to have happen'. Omar assisted in the construction of the Truth and Reconciliation Commission and he claims that in the South African case, the issues of amnesty had already been negotiated before the first democratic government came into power. It was necessary for South Africans 'to establish accountability in respect of the past' in order 'to establish the rule of law and accountability in the future' (Ibid.).

In all of the preceding examples of global communities coming together to engage as partners in healing, forgiveness and reconciliation, the primary goal was to find a suitable alternative for building their communities on respect and dignity in a way that best suited their histories, as well as their present and future realities.

## Re-examine Discrimination and Prejudice

Another important consideration in engaging in a global community context is to re-examine one's experiences of discrimination and prejudice and one's role as perpetrator on a regular basis. Discrimination and prejudice in any form denies people their right to respect and dignity and behaving in this way towards even one individual is a crime against humanity. This crime is committed in various forms and through a range of covert and overt means. The media has some responsibility in conveying dehumanizing messages. For example, Jack Shaheen's (2007a) documentary *Reel Bad Arabs: How Hollywood Vilifies a People*, illustrates what he calls 'a pattern of stereotypes that robs a people of their humanity'.

This ongoing introspection will act as a monitor to sharpen one's *cultural diversity sensors*. The *cultural diversity sensor* is an internal thought process that enables you to assess if your assumption and/or your response—verbal and non-verbal—is appropriate, respectful and fair. In attempting to activate the cultural diversity sensors, it might be a good idea to begin with questions that examine your attitude and behaviour on discrimination and prejudice. In this regard, you may reflect on the following questions to determine how discrimination and prejudice affected both your own opportunities and those of others with whom you have interacted.

1. What prejudices and biases guide my interactions with others?
2. In what instances have I experienced discrimination and by whom?
3. How did I feel to be the victim of discrimination?
4. Have I discriminated against someone else and in what way?
5. What stereotypes do I subscribe to and how did I come to 'internalize' these stereotypes?
6. What mental models (psychological representations of reality), according to Eckert (2006), contribute to the perpetuation of stereotypes in my intercultural communication experiences?
7. In exploring my own mental models, what associations do I make when I think about immigrants, the French, brown and black people, people of the Islamic faith, South Asians and Asians in general, the British, indigenous communities and the Americans, for example?
8. In what ways do my mental models inform me in a negative or positive way and influence my behaviour with each of the aforementioned individuals and groups?
9. Have I been the subject of stereotypical behaviour and how did the stereotype obstruct my access to equal opportunities?

In re-examining our mental models and stereotypical behaviours, we may find that we have either subscribed to or been victims of discrimination and prejudice. This awareness allows us to face our demons and to re-assess where we are positioned in the diversity circle. It also allows us to ask questions such as: are we inside the boundary, outside the boundary or are we on the periphery? The answers to these questions would be a good indicator of how we need to make a shift and in which direction, depending on our personal life goals, our workplace requirements and what we consider to be our ultimate life journey. In other words, to decide where to best position ourselves in the diversity circle, we need to develop our diversity consciousness at a deep level through the abovementioned critical processes. While the steps in this process may appear complex, they are not insurmountable as you strive towards achieving a degree of diversity development for meaningful engagement in the global community.

# Engage in Diversity Development

Diversity is understood and defined in a number of different ways across a broad spectrum of individuals, groups, organizations and institutions. In most instances, diversity is regarded as dealing with differences. The differences are observed through culture, language, race and gender. These differences are emphasized and regarded as negative and undesirable. However, diversity is a broader concept and we should take cognizance of this fact by acknowledging the similarities and positive aspects of diversity. Diversity should be regarded as a factor that enhances the overall quality of life bringing a rich blend of ideas and perspectives together.

Given its multidimensional nature, the term diversity is open to a myriad of interpretations and applications all around the world. In some cases, diversity is as narrow as the colour of a person's skin, the languages spoken other than English, and ethnic food and clothing preference. However, diversity is often understood as difference and often in intercultural communication discussions, diversity is specifically about people with different skin colour, languages, customs and habits, and dress codes. A broader reference point of diversity includes religion, gender, ability and disability, sexual orientation and demographic locations. Often, the emphasis in defining and interpreting diversity is focused on differences, shortcomings and inadequacies. O'Hair, Freidrich and Dixon (2008: 60) agree that diversity is 'used to explain how people differ' and the differences are used as a basis for discrimination. However, diversity should be regarded as a variation of sorts, an array of possible options, and a host of opportunities to engage in a fair and open public sphere. Notwithstanding, it is important to note that both similarities and differences in diversity should be celebrated in a positive spirit as a contribution to building the global community.

Diversity development is also about acceptance of diversity as an important contribution to the life of any organization. To this end, it is an enriching experience that allows individuals and groups to grow and flourish together in respect and dignity. According to O'Hair, Friedrich and Dixon (2008: 74), respect for self and others is embodied in the belief that others have a right to differ in opinion, behave as they will, to be treated fairly, and 'not to be ridiculed'.

In exploring the notion of diversity development, we propose the *diversity circle* as another model through which to view diversity development as a gradual development through various phases of growth and enhancement.

The *diversity circle* has three layers: the outer layer comprises the *uncertain phase or the observer status phase* where the individual or group remains outside the circle without any visible or tangible commitment to engaging in diversity. The periphery is the phase at which the individual or group is positioned on the border or the margin of the circle and is best described as the *fence-sitter phase*, while the inner layer of the circle is considered the *immersion phase* during which time the individual or group is actively engaged in diversity, committed to diversity goals and accepts responsibility and accountability for behaviour. (See Figure 4.1)

The *uncertain phase* is characterized by a sceptical approach to diversity development. However, it is an important phase of awareness and consciousness raising, where individuals seek information on ways in which to understand and appreciate diversity. This phase could prove useful in recognizing who one is before making an attempt to know others and it may even assist one in confronting fears and stereotypes. The *fence-sitter phase* is identified through the individual's reluctance to enter the inner circle. But at the same time, it is noted by positive gestures to enter the circle on some occasions and to participate in critical reflection of self and an individual's assumptions. The critical reflective phase helps an individual to re-evaluate his/her persona and reconstruct who they are and want to be. The *immersion phase* is clearly visible when the individual is passionate about making a positive contribution through active, innovative and proactive processes and

**FIGURE 4.1:** Diversity Circle

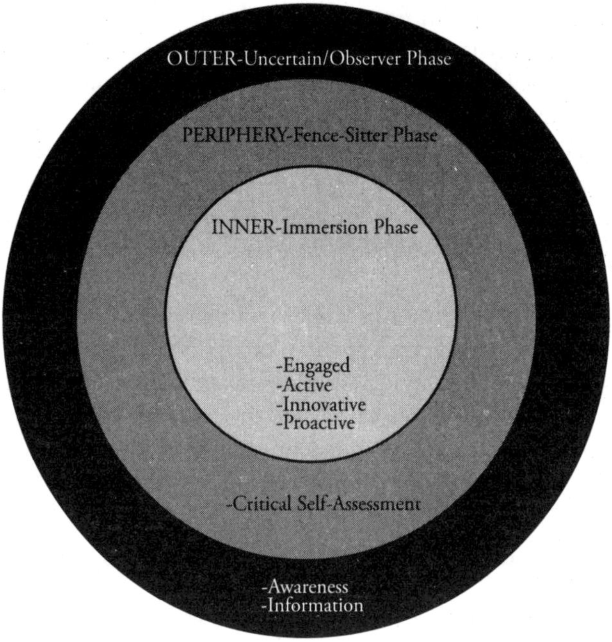

OUTER-Uncertain/Observer Phase

PERIPHERY-Fence-Sitter Phase

INNER-Immersion Phase

-Engaged
-Active
-Innovative
-Proactive

-Critical Self-Assessment

-Awareness
-Information

Illustration by Farhaan Patel.

actions to enhance diversity. This is the transformational phase when one observes a development in attitude, intercultural competencies, judgements and application of knowledge about diversity. In summary, it is important to note that there are several phases in developing diversity: awareness, recognition, confrontation, reflection, reconstruction and transformation. All these are important phases and there is no time-frame on how long or short each phase might be.

Responsibility for diversity rests squarely on everyone's shoulders. It demands commitment to social justice issues, social responsibility and inclusive spaces. The ultimate or *immersion phase* ensures commitment to diversity to the degree that it moves the discourse away from the 'us versus them' mindset and the notion of 'accommodation and special treatment'. This critical phase enhances and raises the quality of diversity development from design and implementation to a critical review of the diversity experience for all stakeholders.

Diversity development is a positive notion that is process-oriented and reflects the ongoing circle of events. It continues to evolve over time, respond to current and future needs and offers innovative and creative ideas for global community engagement. Throughout the various phases of diversity development, individuals and groups implement various strategies and embrace several characteristics of successful global community engagement.

Of course, we have to also immerse ourselves in diversity development initiatives to better understand what diversity means, how we may contribute to a healthy model of diversity and particularly to broaden our knowledge of ourselves within the diversity circle so that we may continuously seek to define and redefine our diversity boundaries.

## Defining Diversity Boundaries

Defining and redefining our diversity boundaries suggests that the individual not only has a right to establish the diversity boundary, but it also indicates that he/she has the power to shift the boundary lines for personal and professional comfort and/or growth. The redefinition of boundaries will involve putting into practice the aforementioned desirable norms of engagement after critical self-analysis on an ongoing basis. Further, this redefinition of boundaries will ensure the expansion of the diversity circle to meet current and future needs.

In the process of re-defining the boundaries of diversity, one must be weary of the promises of the *melting pot policy*, for example. The idea behind this much-touted concept is on reducing differences between people and is therefore inimical to the goal of blurring the lines of differences between them in keeping with the notion of cultural inclusion, as opposed to cultural exclusion. In other words, an ideal world would be one in which all cultures, general and specialized, are encouraged to flourish, yet allowing people to retain their individual identities, thus underscoring the merits of *cultural pluralism*.

# Conclusion

This chapter focused on one's values, beliefs and behaviours to see how these might have to be adapted, modified and negotiated for meaningful and successful global community engagement. Particularly, global community engagement involves the negotiation of selected components of intercultural communication and remains focused on the mutual goal of pursuing the common good for all people. In identifying and discussing the established and desired norms of global community engagement through emphasis on critical self-reflection of one's own biases, prejudices and worldviews, it is hoped that global community engagement becomes a mutually rewarding intercultural communication experience for all the parties in today's increasingly diverse global community.

## Chapter 5

# Education for the Global Citizen

Hinduism: 'This is the sum of duty—do naught unto others which would cause you pain if done to you.' *The Mahabharata, 5:1517*

## Introduction

This chapter discusses the concepts of globalization, explains the meaning of global citizenship, describes the global competencies and identifies the scope of global education. It argues that global education should equip global citizens with adequate knowledge, skills and attitudes to participate in the civic society to address the global challenges, issues and problems they face and build a better future for themselves and for future generations.

We live in an interrelated and interdependent world. Every day the media carries news throughout the world 24/7. We hear debates about many global issues and share differing views on these issues. For example, most people will support increased security measures against terrorist attacks. Some people support the wars in Iraq and in Afghanistan, but some people oppose these military actions. Some may favour a quick response to global warming, but some may not care about it. Some may approve Israeli military actions in the Middle East, but some may oppose them. Western leaders vie with each other to meet with the Dalai Lama to enhance their own personal profiles, but China strongly opposes such meetings, perceiving this as a Western interference with Chinese sovereignty and territorial integrity. Some may support the United States' selling of sophisticated weapons to Taiwan, but some oppose such a move. These issues can only be addressed from a global perspective rather than from a local perspective in the interest of one particular country or region or group or individuals. If one is interested in these issues and wish to find responses to them, one become a global citizen.

*Global citizens*—also called international citizens, or world citizens—has become a buzzword. This chapter explains the meaning of this concept. Education for the global citizen is becoming increasingly important and urgent. To have a better understanding of the concept of global education and its significance, it is important to examine the impacts of globalization on individuals and societies, understand the meaning of global citizenship and global education, the scope of global citizenship education, and the challenges facing global citizens.

# Globalization

Sassen (2006) describes globalization as a process that denationalizes what has been constructed as national; such as policies, capital, industries, information, politics and global ecology. The growth of technology and globalization mutually reinforce each other (Streeten, 2001). Technological progress has reduced the cost of communications and transportation, eliminated geographical and spatial barriers, facilitated the free flow of foreign capital, goods, trade, services, technology, peoples, information, ideas and foreign direct investment (FDI). More transborder data flow through communication satellites, the Internet, wireless telephones, etc. The Internet increases global commonality in consumer needs and tastes and reduces the costs of production and transforms traditional patterns of business and trade management (Fatehi, 2008).

Globalization has brought about many changes in the global business environment. World trade benefits from decreased trade barriers; many countries are striving for free trade, fighting against trade protectionism, and eliminating tariffs, quotas and preferences on most goods and services between trading partners. The aim is to promote economic development and cooperation through free trade agreements, such as North American Free Trade Agreement, the European Union, the Association of Southeast Asian Nations Free Trade Area, the Common Market of Eastern and Southern Africa, the Sino-New Zealand Free Trade Agreement, and New Zealand and Malaysian Free Trade Agreement. Yukio Hatoyama, the Japanese Prime Minister proposed the formation of an EU-style Asian community to promote regional cooperation in East Asia.

Globalization has led to a change in attitude in developing countries towards FDI. Before mid-1970s, developing countries often held negative attitudes toward FDI. Now their attitudes have changed and they are competing with one another to attract FDI through various packages of investment incentives and inducements (Fatehi, 2008). According to Mansoor Dailami, Manager of International Finance, Development Prospects Group of the World Bank, USD 385 billion of USD 1.4 trillion of global FDI flew into developing countries. By 2008, China had remained the first destination of global FDI in developing countries for 17 years, attracting 130 billion capital inflow, more than one-third of the global FDI in developing countries (Correspondent, 2009). The capital flow has encouraged developing countries to adopt export-oriented strategies in their trade policies. For example, China's exports of goods and services constitute nearly forty per cent of its GDP. China's surging trade surplus of USD 159.23 billion with the USA by October 2009 has caused trade tension between the two countries and the USA imposed a series of anti-dumping sanction on Chinese imports (Chung, 2009).

National borders are increasingly losing its effectiveness in managing international business. The number of countries that allow dual citizenship is on the rise and there are calls for 'flexible citizenship' or 'transnationalism' (Fatehi, 2008: 11). Many top executives of well-known American, European and Australasian firms are foreign citizens. Many university academics in these countries are also foreign citizens. An Indian professor may teach at an Australian and New Zealand university; a New Zealand academic may teach at a university in Dubai or Kuwait or Saudi Arabia. Traditional sense of national borders seems to be disappearing. Professor John Hood, a New Zealand citizen, became Vice-Chancellor of the University of Oxford from 5 October 2004 until 30 September 2009. He was the first Vice-Chancellor to be elected from outside Oxford's academic body. Professor Yang Fujia, a Chinese citizen, was formally installed as the University of Nottingham's sixth Chancellor on 4 July 2001; a first time for a Chinese academic becoming Chancellor of a UK university.

The world is moving towards integration and international inter-dependence in many areas, such as trade, finance, direct investment, education, technology, ideology, culture, ecology, environment, law, military, politics and strategies. Concerted effort and cooperation are required to address many of the global issues, such as terrorism, piracy on high seas, AIDS, diseases, the global outbreak of the pandemic H1N1 flu virus, climate change, famine, hunger, starvation and human rights issues. There is an increased level of interconnections and inter-dependence between businesses, corporations, companies, organizations and nation-states. Today, the global village dream has become more realistic. Global interconnections and interdependence require people to apply the concept of citizenship to a global level, instead of at national or regional level.

## Global Citizenship, What does It Mean?

Defining global citizenship is a challenge. Before we make an attempt to explain the meaning of global citizenship, we will first look at the definition and meaning of citizenship. It is our understanding that global citizenship and national citizenship are related but they are also significantly different. Dower and Williams (2002: xix) define citizenship as:

> ...membership, determined by formal factors such as place of birth, parentage or act of naturalisation, or political community (generally a nation-state) by virtue of which one has legally defined rights (including

political rights not necessarily accorded to other residents) and duties, and moral responsibilities to participate in the public life of one's political community.

The notion of citizenship involves an extensive range of issues, such as political, social and cultural rights, responsibilities, social status and attendant privileges (Walat, 2006: 165). The citizen can exercise all the accorded legal and democratic rights to reside, vote, express views, associate with others, enjoy the benefits and travel freely within the entire country. At the same time, the citizen also has duties and responsibilities, such as owing allegiance to a sovereign state, defending national interests, serve in the military, pay taxes, obey laws, and respect authority within a powerful and effective government. Osler (2005) catergorizes citizenship as:

1. a *status* (which confers on the individual the rights to residence, vote, and employment),
2. a *feeling* (sense of belonging to a community) and
3. *practice* (active participation in the building of democratic societies).

O'Byrne (2003) pointed out that there are four components of citizenship: (*a*) membership in terms of a nation-state, (*b*) civil, political and social rights and liberties, (*c*) duties to the state and community within the national boundary and (*d*) participation in national, regional and local affairs and decision-making. As you can see, citizenship is an all-inclusive concept and embraces a multilayered sense of belonging (Garcia, 2006).

A global citizen, however, does not have the rights a national citizen can enjoy. She is not a legal member and does not have freedom to reside, vote, enjoy the benefits and travel freely outside her own nation-state. She does not have clearly recognizable privileges and duties associated with national citizenship. She does not owe any allegiance to a world government or global government that does not exist at all. Scorza (2004: 5) defined the global citizen as 'a person with all of the rights and responsibilities of membership in the human polity and, ideally, also the capabilities needed to fulfil the former and enjoy the latter'.

Therefore, global citizenship entails the rights and responsibilities, that have been listed by Scorza as the following:

1. The right to life, liberty and security of person;
2. rights of due process and equal recognition, freedom from discrimination;
3. freedom of thought, conscience, religion and expression;
4. freedom of association and assembly, and the right to universal suffrage; and
5. rights to property, health, education and a decent standard of living.

Unlike the rights outlined above, the responsibilities are more hypothetical. There are no clear political, theoretical and institutional frameworks to guide one's actions and behaviour. They are associated with one's understanding of the roles, place and relationship to global issues. Scorza (2004: 6) proposed that the responsibilities of global citizenship should include:

1. Respect the rights of others,
2. develop the basic competencies of global citizenship,
3. use these competencies intelligently to do justice to others, and
4. participate in the public affairs of one's country for the sake of justice.

In a similar vein, O'Byrne (2003: 21) identifies a global citizen as a member of a multicultural society whose rights shift from citizenship and civil liberties towards the 'public sphere' of humanity; from the consciousness of a national citizen to the consciousness of belonging to a global community of mankind and whose major focus shifts from national interest to the survival of the planet, from viewing oneself as an individual or a local actor to viewing oneself as an actor of the world, and finally in taking responsibility to address global challenges.

Scorza (2004: 6) states that a global citizen may be a member of any community that is based on the principle of equality and on the concept of citizenship that transcends the state. She is expected to live a global way of life and work effectively anywhere in the world

(Noddings, 2005). She has a sense of belonging in a global community, cares about global issues, gets involved in global politics, social and cultural activities, and develops 'habits of mind, heart, body, and soul that have to do with working for and preserving a network of relationships and connections across lines of difference and distinctness, while keeping and deepening a sense of one's own identity and integrity' (McIntosh, 2005: 23). Lagos (2002) explains that a global citizen is not legally recognized and therefore should be defined by her 'associational' status that is different from national citizenship but free from bureaucratic interventions. Such an 'associational' status often defies national boundaries and sovereignty with its transnational norms and status. Fleming (2006: 140) notes that the global citizen can 'assert some sort of transcendental belonging to a world community', embrace the particular as well as the universal, belong to particular local and national communities and have 'a higher degree of awareness of the contingency of those allegiances'. Fleming further maintains that the global citizen should be able to step outside the perceptual confines and constraints and develop 'an ability to see one's own behaviour and values from "outside"' (Ibid.: 142).

Falk (1994) identifies five categories of global citizens: global reformer, elite global business people, global environmental managers, politically conscious regionalists and transnational activists. In Falk's view, global citizenship can be understood from the five layers explained in the following list.

1. Inspirational orientation in spirit, adhering to a normative perspective to create a better world, to broaden and globalize our outlook, and to achieve global integration, especially economically.
2. Global citizen as a man and woman of transnational affairs, focusing on the impact of globalization of economic forces.
3. Management of the global order in economic and environmental dimensions.
4. Global citizenship that is associated with the rise of regional political consciousness.
5. Global citizenship that is associated with the emergence of transnational activism.

Lagos (2002) notes that global citizens are people who travel within these various layers or boundaries and claim the rights accorded by the citizens themselves and by the general public in favour of 'universal rights'. Lagos (2002: 9) emphasized that that a national citizenship is more closed and a global citizenship is more flexible and inclusive.

Global means planetary, but as Byers (2005: 2) explains, it can also mean local, individual and personal:

> Global could mean spherical, well-rounded, so that describing someone as global would mean that they were widely read, holistic in their appreciation of the world around them, and therefore understanding of the situations and perspectives of others. Global could even mean adaptable, like a travel plug for a hairdryer or electronic razor. In this sense, a person who was global could readily fit into various positions, locations, even countries and cultures.

Byers argues that we all dwell in two communities: the local community of our birth and the broader community beyond our national border. Global citizenship is formed on the basis of the values of collective responsibility inherent in these two communities, such as environmental protection, human rights, democracy, peace, freedom, dignity and justice. Byers (2005: 8) concludes that:

> Global citizenship empowers individual human beings to participate in decisions concerning their lives, including the political, economic, social, cultural and environmental conditions in which they live... It is expressed through engagement in the various communities of which the individual is a part, at the local, national and global level. It includes the right to challenge authority and existing power structures, to think, argue and act with the intent of changing the world.

Global citizenship, as can be seen from the above discussion, is not confined to one discipline and to nation-states. The global citizen needs to be equipped with some core competencies to transcend national and cultural boundaries and engage with the global community in global activities.

# The Global Citizen and Global Competencies

Global citizens face many complex and pressing global issues and challenges that require them to take individual and social responsibilities to recognize and address these trends and issues that affect each personally. To meet such challenges of global issues, they need to develop three dimensions of skills: knowledge, motivation and behaviour (Neuliep, 2006). Scorza (2004: 6) suggests that a global citizen should develop the following competencies:

1. Knowledge of world geography, current world affairs and the role of one's country in the world;
2. critical thinking, collaborative skills and cross-cultural skills; and
3. attitudes such as curiosity, open-mindedness and empathy.

Global citizens need to develop intellectual and critical abilities to grapple effectively and meaningfully with critical global issues. They need to apply the knowledge of these issues, based on their understanding of the current international context in relation to local and global stakeholders, and be motivated to engage with local and global communities to serve the values and ethical norms of global citizenship. To achieve such a goal, some core global competencies are required and need to be nurtured. Kubow, Grossman and Ninomiya (1998: 132) identified eight core competencies that should be cultivated. These are as follows:

1. The ability to look at and approach problems as a member of a global society.
2. The ability to work with others in a cooperative way and to take responsibility for one's roles/duties within society.
3. The ability to understand, accept, appreciate and tolerate cultural differences.
4. The capacity to think in a critical and systemic way.
5. The willingness to resolve conflict in a non-violent manner.
6. The willingness to change one's lifestyle and consumption habits to protect the environment.

7. The ability to be sensitive towards and to defend human rights, like rights of women, ethnic minorities, etc.
8. The willingness and ability to participate in politics at local, national and international levels.

Scorza (2004: 15) identifies four perspectives of global competencies that a global citizen needs to develop: global, individual, cross-cultural and experience. In the global perspective, Scorza maintains that the global citizen needs to become familiar with the complexity of global issues, including economic, environmental, health and population concerns, apply knowledge to address these concerns, understand what it means to be a global citizen, and use technology for research, communication and community building. In the individual perspective, a global citizen needs to have the ability to 'examine numerous personal philosophies and value systems incorporating ideas from multi-disciplinary perspectives' (Ibid:. 16). In the cross-cultural perspective, a global citizen needs to become familiar with multiple cultural perspectives, examine and deconstruct inherent ethnocentrism in light of these perspectives, and engage in a comparative analysis of complex social, economic and political structures (Ibid.: 16). In the experience perspective, according to him (Ibid.: 16), a global citizen needs to have 'the ability to integrate knowledge of the world, the personal self and other cultures in a capstone course', examine one's own cultural norms and practice and critically evaluate one's own cultural perceptions. All of these four perspectives require seven core competencies:

1. Ability to be thoughtful, open-minded and curious;
2. to live with the complexity, ambiguity and difficulty of modern life;
3. to participate responsibly and effectively in multiple communities (including the global community);
4. to integrate multiple bodies of knowledge to help solve complex problems;
5. to integrate discursive and non-discursive (e.g., music, art) forms of expression;
6. to participate in an ongoing common intellectual discourse without fear or prejudice; and
7. to practice critical thinking, writing and interpretation.

Neuliep (2006) emphasizes that a competent global citizen needs to understand verbal and non-verbal scripts. Verbal scripts include language in the form of writing and speaking. Ability to speak another foreign language would facilitate a global citizen's knowledge of another culture and the world. It is not difficult to find examples to illustrate this point. For instance, in Luxembourg, a a trilingual country, German, French and Luxembourgish are official languages. When children begin to speak, they speak Luxembourgish. When they go to the kindergarten, they are taught to speak the other two official languages—German and French. When they enter the secondary school, they begin to learn English and Latin. German and French are the languages used by the mass media. French and Luxembourgish are used in parliament debates. Luxembourgish is used in the court trial and English to announce the verdict, while the court documents are written in German. In one family, it may not be surprising if you see the father reading a German-language newspaper, the son reading a French-language book, the daughter singing an English song and the mother talking in Luxembourgish. It is obvious that the ability to speak one or two or more foreign languages and the ability to understand non-verbal scripts would help the global citizen broaden her vision, enhance cross-cultural understanding, facilitate her active participation in global affairs and function effectively and constructively in today's interconnected world.

Neuliep (2006) also suggests that the global citizen should develop the ability to examine one's ethnocentric attitudes, racism and racial discrimination. Ethnocentrism can be understood as the tendency to evaluate and interpret other cultures according to one's own standards, to place one's own group in a position of centrality and worth, and create negative attitudes and behaviours toward other groups. It tends to be self-destructive. It deters interaction with others, rejects new ideas and leads to racism and racial discrimination. Awareness of racial discrimination and determination to eliminate it may be viewed as an important global competence.

Ethnocentrism, racism and racial discrimination are very often subliminally implicit. People who discriminate against other ethnicities may reject any accusation of being racist. Many Chinese people would refuse to accept that racism and racial discrimination exist in China. Three incidents that happened in China sparked a series of intense nation-wide debates about Chinese national identity—skin colour. A 20-year-old Shanghai girl, Luo Jing, became exceptionally popular on the Internet after her appearance on Dragon TV's *Oriental Angels* in August 2009. A torrent of abusive language and racist remarks was used to attack her on the Internet when many netizens learned that she was born after her married mother had extra-marital relations with an African-American father whom she had never met. The colour of her skin became a target of attack. A second incident took place in Shanghai in November 2009. A 20-year-old woman gave birth to a mixed-race baby girl. Having relations with a black man was considered a disgrace to the family and as a result her parents disowned her. The third event that caused Chinese soul-searching and dialogue on racism was US President Obama's state visit to China in November 2009. To many young Chinese, President Obama is a symbol of ideals of equality, a vast contrast to the reality in China where skin colour and family backgrounds similar to Obama's had caused outright racism and discrimination. Many Chinese people, having grown up and been educated in a fairly ethnically homogenous society, have begun to examine the many sensitive and global issues in relation to ethnocentrism, racism and racial discrimination. As China continues to open up to the outside world, interactions with foreign citizens in China will be prevalent. Thousands of foreign citizens are doing business in China. For instance, the African community in China has grown dramatically since China joined the World Trade Organisation in 2001, with as many as 250,000 in the country (Duncan, 2009) as well as, about a 100,000-strong community of African traders in Guangzhou. Mixed-race marriages are becoming more and more popular. In Shanghai alone, more than 3,000 mixed-race marriages are registered every year (Canaves and Oster, 2009). The social, cultural and economic changes and demographic shifts have prompted the Chinese citizens to seriously confront racism and discrimination for the first time.

## Definition and Scope of Global Education

It is worth noting that effective global education is the only way to equip global citizens with global competencies to effectively deal with personal, local, national and international issues and problems. What is education for global citizenship? Like global citizenship, there is no universally acceptable definition of global education available in literature today. As Merryfield (1993: 28) maintains, it is 'one of the more ambiguous innovations in education today'. Different scholars look at the concept from different perspectives. Lack of a consensus on the definition and the ambiguity of existing definitions from the literature reflects the complexity and interdisciplinary inclusiveness of the concept, and as Roux (2001: 73) argues, it offers 'an opportunity for a teacher's flexibility, innovation and creativity in implementing a global education perspective into the classroom whilst taking political, economic, demographic, social and cultural realities into consideration at the same time'. Global education, according to Ikeda (1996: 2), is 'a uniquely human privilege…the source of inspiration that enables us to become fully and truly human, to fulfil a constructive mission in life with composure and confidence'.

Tye and Tye (1992: 6) define global education as 'the study of problems and issues that cut across national boundaries, and the interconnectedness of the systems involved…[and] the cultivation of cross-cultural understanding, which includes development of skill of perspective-taking' and seeing the world through the eyes and minds of others. Similarly, Kniep (1989) states that global education should take into consideration global issues and problems, human value, global systems and global history. Calder and Smith (1993: 18) identify global education as 'a dynamic process, which leads to a critical awareness and sensitivity regarding real life issues…[and] motivates students to social action'. Case (1993) suggests that global education involves an orientation of worldview and knowledge of the world and how it works. Calder (2000: 82) notes that global education should focus on four dimensions: (*a*) global concerns in this interdependent world, including the factors that cause poverty, injustice, inhumanity and conflict; (*b*) powerful and powerless, involving prejudice, racism, discrimination and sexism; (*c*) critical awareness of own society and culture and that of others; and (*d*) participation and commitment to responsible action for change. To Simmons and Strenecky (1996), global education is designed to develop global citizens' awareness, understanding, familiarity and appreciation of global issues and events, other cultures, global interconnectedness and interdependence. The purpose of global education, as can be inferred from these definitions, is to equip global citizens with knowledge and competencies to cope with emerging global realities and new demands in this rapidly changing world (Case, 1993). Common goals of global education should include the following features:

1. Understanding of global interrelatedness and interdependence,
2. respecting cultural diversity,
3. fighting racial discrimination,
4. protecting the global environment,
5. understanding human rights, and
6. accepting basic social values.

These six major goals of global education are not mutually exclusive. They are mutually inclusive, with one relating to another. Of course, they do not exclude other goals, such as participation in civic activities, dimensions of change, social justice, peace building and sustainable future, frameworks for teaching in schools and universities, the learning process and professional development in terms of global education. This chapter, for its brevity, will discuss the six major goals.

## Understanding of Global Interrelatedness and Interdependence

We all live in an interdependent world. The problems we face are complex, multi-dimensional and global. Solutions cannot be sought at the local level. We cannot survive if we think and act solely on a nation-based mentality. Global education seeks to prepare students to live in the 'global village' and to be active participants to shape a better future (*Global Perspectives*, 2005). A global citizen needs to acknowledge and recognize the interrelatedness and interdependence in a neighbourhood, a town, a state, a nation and the world. The interdependence, fuelled by the Internet and telecommunications technologies can be seen in almost all spheres, such as economy, finance, trade and investment, migration, tourism, security, international education, public health, global governance and environmental concerns. Globalization has brought about growing international contacts. For example, in 2008, 543,898 international students were enrolled in education programmes in Australia (Studies in Australia, n.d.). Australian international education, also called export education, contributes 14 billion Australian dollars to the Australian economy and creates 122,000 FTE (Full-time Equivalency) positions, plus 126,240 FTE positions associated with student-related expenditure (spending by students and visiting friends and relatives) (Access Economics, 2009). In New Zealand, prior to the passage of the 1989 Education Act, international students were an exotic rarity in New Zealand schools and universities. However, in 10 years time, the number of first time student visas issued to fee paying international students rose from 8,233 in 1998/99 to 30,726 in 2008/09 and the $2 billion export industry generates 45,000 FTE position for New Zealanders (Stevens, 2010).

We must realize that we are confronted with global issues and problems. The polluted air and the climate change affect all of us. The AIDS virus and H1N1 swine flu can travel anywhere they will. Not a single economy can pretend that it has not been affected by the impact of the financial crises and the economic recession. News of the 2010 Haiti and Chile earthquakes reached the listeners, readers and viewers in all corners of the globe in a very short time through the Internet and telecommunication systems, and international aids and donations poured in soon afterwards. Also, Global terrorism and Somali pirates touch our nerves. The 9/11 attack on the World Trade Center suggests that we are not immune to terrorism. Collective and concerted efforts are needed to resolve many global issues and problems. Global education seeks to foster within learners perspective-taking and 'empathy for the lived experience of diverse communities, and to encourage active participation in devising strategies and solutions for the future' (*Global Perspectives*, 2005: 5).

## Respecting Cultural Diversity

The people of the world come from different races and different cultural backgrounds. They are different in skin colour, eye and hair colour, language, religion, values, beliefs, assumptions, traditions, nationality, behaviour, festivals and celebrations, ideas, thoughts, socio-political and economic systems, and ways of communication. We live a world of cultural diversity which enriches our lives and helps people respect one another's contribution to the advancement of the world. We all have universal basic feelings and emotions, such as love, joy, surprise, fear, anger and sadness (Shaver et al., 2001: 36). The statement by Shylock, a fictional character in Shakespeare's play *The Merchant of Venice* (Act 3, Scene 1, 58–68) suggests that under the skin, we are all the same:

> I am a Jew. Hath not a Jew eyes? Hath not a Jew hands, organs, dimensions, senses, affections, passions; fed with the same food, hurt with the same weapons, subject to the same diseases, heal'd by the same means, warm'd and cool'd by the same winter and summer, as a Christian is? If you prick us, do we not bleed? If you tickle us, do we not laugh? If you poison us, do we not die? And if you wrong us, do we not revenge? If we are like you in the rest, we will resemble you in that.

The *UNESCO Universal Declaration on Cultural Diversity* (2001) sees cultural diversity as the common heritage of humanity, a source of identity, exchange, innovation and creativity, and therefore it 'should be recognized and affirmed for the benefit of present and future generations' (Article 1). Cultural diversity forms a democratic framework for inclusion, solidarity and participation by all citizens 'as a means to achieve more satisfactory intellectual, emotional, moral and spiritual existence' (Article 3). The Declaration affirms that respect for cultural diversity, tolerance, dialogue and cooperation, mutual trust and understanding guarantee international peace and security, social cohesion, and the development of economy.

To promote cultural diversity, the New Zealand Human Right Commission initiated and facilitated the NZ Diversity Programme in 2004, following the desecration of two Jewish cemeteries in Wellington in July and August of the year. The programme brings together 250 organizations with 661 projects to recognize and celebrate the cultural diversity of the society, promote the equal enjoyment of human rights and foster harmonious relations between diverse peoples (NZ Human Rights Commission, 2010). March 21 is designated as Race Relations

Day in New Zealand—an international day for eliminating racial discrimination. Forums have been held, featuring cultural, religious and language diversity, current issues, politics, the Treaty of Waitangi, media literacy, health, education, employment and refugee issues.

## Fighting Racial Discrimination

Fighting racial discrimination is a tough and long ongoing battle. Racial discrimination, based on skin colour, nationality, ethnicity and language erodes the social fabric of the society. It exists in many societies in various forms:

1. Direct and deliberate discrimination: Verbal abuse, assault and policy that denies the rights of certain ethnic groups.
2. Indirect discrimination: Working practice and criteria that are set to disadvantage some ethnic groups. For example, members of certain ethnic groups may not be promoted in the workplace in spite of their satisfactory performance.
3. Harassment: Behaviour and practices that intend to offend some members of ethnic groups, workplace bullying, racist jokes.

Job applicants, if their names are perceived as 'sounding foreign' may be less likely to have access to employment than candidates perceived as having 'white-sounding' names (Li and Campbell, 2009).

According to an UMR research poll conducted in December 2009 for the New Zealand Human Rights Commission, respondents were asked to name groups of people who they think are generally most discriminated against in New Zealand: 28 per cent said Asians for their first mention, 13 per cent said Pakeha, 10 per cent said Māori and 5 per cent said Pacific peoples (New Zealand Human Rights Commission, 2010: 15). Asians were believed to be the largest group (75 per cent), compared to Pacific peoples (58 per cent) and Māori (56 per cent), that suffers a great deal or some discrimination. Reasons for discrimination include colour skin, nationality, race or ethnic group, language, dress and appearance.

The annual report by New Zealand Human Rights Commission (2010: 15) states that '10 per cent of New Zealanders experienced discrimination. The most common grounds were nationality, race, ethnic group or skin colour. Asians experienced the most discrimination.' The report said that many racially motivated crimes, harassment and assaults were reported in the news media in 2009 and racial disharmony was considered to be a serious issue that needed to be addressed. For example, Jae Hyeon Kim, a Korean backpacker, was killed in Nelson in 2003 by Hayden Mckenzie, a race-hate murderer. An Indo-Fujian student was attacked in Christchurch in August 2009. An Indian taxi driver was assaulted and humiliated and his turban was removed by four passengers in Auckland in April 2009.

Such racially inspired crimes and assaults are also reported in Australia. In Victoria State alone, in the year ending in July 2008, police reported that 1,447 Indians have been mugged, knifed, set alight, assaulted and murdered (Marks, 2010). The relationship between Australia and India has been soured after a spate of serious attacks on Indian citizens, mostly in Melbourne. The number of Indians applying for overseas student visa fell 46 per cent for the period from July to 31 October 2009, compared with the same period in 2008 (Harrison, 2010).

Racial discrimination is also a serious social issue in the United States. According to the *2008 Hate Crime Statistics* released by the FBI (2008), 7,783 criminal incidents involving 9,168 offences were reported in 2008. Of those, 51.3 per cent were motivated by racial bias, 19.5 per cent by religious bias and 11.5 per cent by ethnicity/national origin bias. Among those hate crimes:

1. 72.6 per cent were against black people;
2. 65.7 per cent were anti-Jewish;
3. 64.0 per cent were due to anti-Hispanic bias;
4. 36.0 per cent were because of anti-other ethnicity/national origin bias.

The Southern Poverty Law Center (n.d.) in the United States issued a *Hate Map*, detailing the racist hate groups in the country in an environment of racial intolerance and ethnic hatred. It counted 932 active hate groups in the United States in 2009. The activities of racist hate groups, based on their racist beliefs, include criminal activity and violence.

## Protecting the Global Environment

Environmental degradation does not carry any passport and knows no national boundaries. It is not a national problem; it is a global one. The environmental challenges we face transcend national borders. The list of problems is enormous. They include unchecked population growth, depletion of the ozone layer, acid rain, deforestation, hazardous wastes and chemicals, endangered species, marine pollution, severe shortages of usable fresh water, resource depletion, destruction of arable lands, disposal of nuclear and chemical waste, erosion, salination of the soil and climate change. At this critical juncture, *The Earth Charter*, a declaration of fundamental ethical values and principles, calls upon humanity to take a collective responsibility and 'join together to bring forth a sustainable global society founded on respect for nature, universal human rights, economic justice, and a culture of peace' (Earth Charter Commission, Preamble, 2009).

Snyder (1995: 85) argues that environmental problems and social conflicts are systematically intertwined, each being the cause of the other, leading to the 'lethal spiral', a dangerous cycle that threatens human survival. He reasons that population growth can cause concentration and displacement and then puts burdens on the environment in various forms: pollution, depletion of water and deforestation. In the end, there appears to be an ecological crisis, which in turn leads to social conflict as a result of famine, disease, migration, religious and political tensions. Social conflict can aggravate environmental problems and cause further population growth. Kaplan (1994: 44) warns that if the spiral cannot be broken, the environmental problems can become national and international security issues when 'scarcity, crime, overpopulation, tribalism, and disease are rapidly destroying the social fabric of our planet'. Cogan (1998) concludes that environmental problems could lead to the tension between the 'have' and the 'have-not' nations, as a result of immigration pressures and overpopulation in non-industrialized nations. We must work together to find solutions to protect the global environment and promote sustainable development. *The Earth Charter* (Preamble) urges us to take universal responsibility to protect the environment and our future:

To realize these aspirations, we must decide to live with a sense of universal responsibility, identifying ourselves with the whole Earth community as well as our local communities. We are at once citizens of different nations and of one world in which the local and global are linked. Everyone shares responsibility for the present and future well-being of the human family and the larger living world.

## Understanding Human Rights

In 1948, the Universal Declaration of Human Rights (UDHR) first recognized universal and core values of human rights that are inherent to all in the international community. These core values apply to everyone everywhere, and transcend cultures and traditions. They include equality, fairness, non-discrimination, rights and freedoms, dignity, justice, liberty and security, prevention of torture, cruel inhuman degrading treatment and punishment. The UDHR and the concept of the inherent human dignity and worth of every person in the world, without distinction of any kind, cover a wide range of human rights and have been universally accepted. Global education should equip citizens with a thorough understanding of these core values so that they can uphold these universal principles in a world threatened by racial, economic and religious divides. We need to become aware that while we claim, defend and fight for human rights, we should also respect the human rights of other people. While we enjoy human rights, we need to become aware that there are millions of people who do not have such good luck. Here are some facts provided by Shah (2009):

1. At least 80 per cent of humanity lives on less than $10 a day.
2. Twenty-five thousand children die each day due to poverty.
3. An estimated 40 million people are living with HIV/AIDS.
4. Every year there are 350–500 million cases of malaria, with 1 million fatalities. Africa accounts for 90 per cent of malarial deaths and African children account for over 80 per cent of malaria victims worldwide.
5. Some 1.1 billion people in developing countries have inadequate access to water and 2.6 billion lack basic sanitation.

6. Around 2.2 million children die each year because they are not immunized.
7. The world's wealthiest countries (approximately 1 billion people) account for $36.6 trillion dollars (76 per cent).
8. Approximately 790 million people in the developing world are still chronically undernourished, almost two-thirds of whom reside in Asia and the Pacific.

Cases of human rights violations—the terrible practices of ethnic cleansing, religious persecution, racism, inequality, torture, gender-based oppression, violence against women, massacre, genocide, inhuman treatment, sexual mutilation, sexual humiliation, political oppression, child labour and slavery—have been reported in every continent. Keven Bales (2004) reported in his book *Disposal People: New Slavery in the Global Economy* that there were 10s of millions of slaves, or what he called 'disposal people', in our civilized world. Millions of people have been, and are being, persecuted, tortured and killed (Abdi, 2008). On 7 March 2010, at least 200 Christian villagers in central Nigeria were murdered (Human Rights Watch, 2010). In April 1992, an estimated 350 Bosnian Muslim men were tortured to death and massacred by Serb paramilitaries and special police (Jones, n.d.). On 18 July 1995, the Bosnian Serb army had systematically executed thousands of Muslim women and children. The remainder were deported from the area westwards into Muslim-held territory. The Red Cross lists 7,079 dead and missing at Srebrenica (Ibid.).

The 'Human Rights Record of the United States in 2009' issued by the State Council of the Republic of China (2010) indicates that the wars of Iraq and Afghanistan launched by the United States have brought tremendous casualties and property losses to the people of both countries. The war in Iraq has led to the deaths of more than one million Iraqi civilians and rendered an equal number of people homeless. Charles (2008) reported that there was strong evidence to suggest that 11 former terrorism suspects held by US troops at Guantanamo Bay on Cuba had been physically, psychologically and sexually mistreated. The mistreatment included beatings and other physical and sexual abuse, isolation, forced nakedness and being forced into painful stress positions with their hands and feet bound. The interrogation techniques included 'waterboarding'—simulated drowning. Similarly in Iraq, the United States and its private contractors tortured detained male Muslims in Iraq by stacking the naked prisoners in pyramid formation, coercing homosexual behaviours and stripping them in stark nakedness ('Human Rights Record of the United States in 2009').

## Accepting Basic Social Values

Citizenship is in essence a social activity although individual qualities are important (Kubow, Grossman and Ninomiya, 1998). The core values outlined in the Universal Declaration of Human Rights can be used as a guideline to our civic behaviour. Social involvement becomes an important element in global education. A global citizen should be able to interact, communicate and work together with other people from different socio-cultural settings and contexts. Participation in a variety of civic activities and local socialization makes global education possible. Such civic engagement and involvement in a civic society requires citizens to accept basic social values as guiding principles in their social interaction, and at the same time to form certain sets of attitudes. The Australian global education guideline, *Global Perspectives: A Framework for Global Education in Australian Schools* (2008: 6) lists eight values and attitudes to be cultivated:

1. A sense of personal identity and self-esteem.
2. A sense of community with the people around the world.
3. Caring and compassionate concern for others.
4. A recognition of shared responsibilities and a willingness to cooperate with others in fulfilling them.
5. A commitment to upholding the rights and dignity of all people.
6. A positive attitude towards diversity and difference.
7. A willingness to learn from the experience of others.
8. An appreciation of and concern for the environment and a commitment to sustainable practices.

A global citizen should develop a sense of personal identity and self-esteem. An individual with high self-esteem is willing and courageous enough to take steps to identify herself with others, with local, national and international communities. One's identity is relative; it exists only when it is associated with others. For example, a student's identity is related to the school, to teachers and other fellow students. Kubow, Grossman and Ninomiya (1998) assert that we all develop multi-dimensional identities which entail many roles to play within several overlapping communities. Multidimensional citizenship suggests that global education should help citizens understand their multiple roles at different levels, from local to multinational, and provide them with skills to empower them to cross cultural and geographical boundaries. Therefore, a citizen needs to develop a sense of belonging. Working with others requires commitments to environmental sustainable development, understanding, caring and passionate concerns for others, and willingness to share responsibilities and appreciate other's experience and diversity.

## Conclusion

Globalization has an enormous impact on all aspects of our life. We are moving towards a world of integration and interdependence. Global interconnections suggest that we must extend our existing concept of national citizenship to a global level and see ourselves as global citizens instead of a local or national citizen. Unlike a national citizen who is associated with legal rights, duties and moral responsibilities, a global citizen is a person who views the world from a global perspective, perceives oneself as an integral part of the world, transcends the national borders, belongs to a global community, seeks to explore and find solutions to global issues and problems, and takes humanity rather than individuals into consideration. A global citizen, in Rene Dubos' well-known dictum, 'thinks globally and acts locally'.

Being an effective global citizen requires a global education. It is through education that citizens begin to develop core competencies to enable them to undertake their moral responsibilities as global citizens. The scope of global education includes the understanding of global interdependence, respecting cultural diversity, fighting racial discrimination, fighting for human rights, accepting basic social or civic values and protecting the environmental degradation to achieve the level of sustainable development. Global education will empower citizens to approach and address problems in a non-violent manner as a member of a global society, think critically and in a systematic way, develop sensitivity to cultural and human rights issues, and to effectively participate in civic activities at local, national and international levels. Educating global citizens to meet global challenges in this rapidly changing world has become an urgent and imperative issue.

## Chapter 6

# Intercultural Communication in the Global Workplace

Judaism: 'What is hateful to you, do not do to your neighbour: that is the whole of the Torah; all the rest is commentary.' *Talmud, Shabbat, 31a*

## Introduction

Today's global economy can best be characterized as an international system of economic interdependence whereby many countries have come together to transact or engage in 'business beyond borders'. Trading of goods and services has become reciprocal as no country is self-sufficient. This changing atmosphere, particularly in an age of globalization, has witnessed a growing pattern of acquisitions, alliances and mergers for economic survival. This dramatic change, however, has had a profound impact on the global workplace as evidenced by an increasingly diverse workforce. As a result, corporations are becoming more culturally sensitive to this global environment due to foreign competition and the need for businesses to survive. It is not surprising, therefore, that the need for effective intercultural communication skills in the global workplace is of paramount importance among its diverse stakeholders.

This chapter begins with a description of general dimensions of culture before examining how culture, gender, race and ethnicity impact workplace communication. It also discusses issues of cultural and racial discrimination, current trends in global workplace communication, diversity in communication styles, barriers to intercultural communication and strategies to enhance intercultural communication. These discussions make reference to global workplace communication—including verbal and non-verbal communication as well as organizational policies and practices—from the mid-twentieth century to the present time through a review of situational examples, research and case studies from Britain, South Africa, the USA, Canada, New Zealand and Australia. To this end, reference would be made as to whether the understanding of intercultural communication has changed and in what ways; what measures have been taken to improve intercultural workplace relationships; and how these measures have contributed to effective workplace communication today.

# General Dimensions of Culture

Global workplace culture and communication must not only be understood within the context of the broad range of research done over decades on the general dimensions of culture, but must also be carefully analysed within the framework of examining one's own culture as noted in other chapters of this book. Before we attempt to understand and analyse other cultural groups, it is essential to first analyse and understand the core values and beliefs of one's own culture. Only then can research on the general dimensions of culture be rationally and pragmatically applied, if and when appropriate.

Much of the research over the decades, particularly in the 1960s to 1980s, focused on cultural behaviour patterns which have been cited countless times in the literature. It is therefore important to note that research on intercultural communication is, not only dated but also biased towards a Western worldview. Nonetheless, the literature is also cited here to provide a broad overview of research done on the general dimensions of culture. At the same time, however, we ask readers to take a critical view of the context of such research. Specifically, we ask that readers self-reflect on their own contextual frameworks before adopting such information and using it in a stereotypical manner. The information presented here provides opportunities for critical self-reflection.

Cultural behaviour patterns that have received much attention over the decades include Hall's high- and low-context cultural taxonomy and Hofstede's (1980) cultural taxonomy. While Hall (1976) and Hofstede (1980) give us an idea of cultural messaging, group behaviour, time orientation, gender preferences, power differentials and collectivist and individualist perspectives, their research is based on the assumption that cultural groups are homogenous. This obliterates the uniqueness of individual and group contributions to the overall cultural pattern. It also perpetuates the stereotyping of cultures and cultural groups and places the burden of responsibility for effective intercultural communication on the external cultural. In order to obtain a better understanding of the general dimensions of culture, one must examine it in the broader context of gender, race and ethnicity.

## Culture, Gender, Race and Ethnicity

A review of culture, gender, race and ethnicity suggests that their impact on intercultural communication has been of special interest and concern for researchers (Samovar and Porter, 2003; Suderman, 2007; O'Hair, Friedrich and Dixon, 2008). While these factors interact with each other in intercultural communication encounters, the degree of interaction varies depending on the communication context and the complexity of the encounter. Among the numerous definitions, Rogers and Steinfatt (1999) define culture as a total way of life of a people, composed of their learned and shared behaviour patterns, values, norms and material objects. One of the key forms of cultural expressions is through communication using symbolic language for shared meaning. In other words, language—verbal and non-verbal—as a medium plays an important role in conveying acceptable and unacceptable messages among people from diverse backgrounds. However, while language is the primary medium through which aspects of culture are expressed, the sender and the recipient may interpret the message in different ways based on their unique cultural gaze (Klyukanov, 2005: 86). Gudykunst and Kim (1997: 13) claim that 'culture influences our communication and that our communication influences culture'. Dodd (1995), on the other hand, suggests that our culture, personality and our perceptions of interpersonal relationships together contribute to the overall communication and that communication emphasizes culture. How one expresses oneself through the medium of spoken language is intricately linked in one's cultural behaviour, beliefs and attitudes. According to Hall (1976: 16):

> Culture is man's medium: there is not one aspect of human life that is not touched and altered by culture. This means personality, how people express themselves (including shows of emotion), the way they think, how they move, how problems are solved, how their cities are planned and laid out, how transportation systems function and are organized, as well as how economic and government systems are put together and function.

Indeed, this comprehensive nature of culture supports the notion that it embraces every aspect of one's life. Another key aspect of culture is gender.

Gender is a 'culturally constructed' label according to Wood (2001: 61) and women and men's roles and behaviour in a society are viewed and valued differently (O'Hair, Freindrich and Dixon, 2008). As in every social context, gender continues to hold a special significance in the global workplace. For example, Magwaza (2009: 10) argues that women's challenges 'in their socio-cultural life get replicated in the domain of the office' and that they are often placed 'at the very bottom of the hierarchy, providing minimal access to positions of authority'.

In what ways, therefore, has the increasing number of women in the marketplace made a difference to how they are perceived and acknowledged in an organization? Miller (2003) claims that although women and people of colour and minorities have entered the workforce in increasing numbers, there is little evidence to suggest that women enjoy equal access and fair treatment. He further contends that women and people of colour are denied access and fair treatment because they are seen to be different. There are systemic barriers within the organization and the presence of gender and cultural bias based on stereotyping and prejudice. As a result, denial of access and fair treatment is of particular relevance to the issue of race.

Today, race is seen more in terms of physical features and varies between and within cultures. For instance, biological and genetic classifications among people even from the same culture accentuate their differences based on the colour of their skin, hair and eyes. Lustig and Koester (1996) claim that race is more political or social in context than it is biological, but may be regarded as a significant factor in negatively influencing communication during intercultural encounters. They further argue that racial differences often are used as the deciding feature to include some individuals in a particular group while excluding others. These groups are classified as ethnic groups and referred to in terms of ethnicity.

Ethnicity refers to ethnic groups which are communal in nature and form their own communities within cultures in a country. According to Samovar and Porter (2003), these ethnic groups share a common origin or heritage including cultural traits such as family names, religion, language and values. They note that a unique feature of ethnicity is that ethnic groups share the 'same social environment' with members of the dominant culture and with other groups. For example, ethnic groups such as Mexicans in San Diego, Haitians in Miami, Indo-Guyanese and East Indians in Queens, New York live in the United States, but retain their respective ethnic cultures. Ongoing cultural practices among members of the ethnic groups help them to preserve their identities while they live within the dominant culture. However, ethnic strife can occur as ethnic groups find it difficult to survive within dominant cultures. In some instances, this struggle for survival has resulted in ethnic groups being victims of ethnic cleansing as in the case of Kosovo, Bosnia and South Africa. These challenges further underscore the tensions regarding race, ethnicity and even gender in intercultural communication.

As a whole, Samovar and Porter (Ibid.: 11) contend that because 'culture is elaborate, abstract and pervasive', there are many aspects of culture that affect communication across cultures. In particular, the influence of culture, race and ethnicity on intercultural communication in the global workplace is an important consideration when analysing issues of access and equity. Janzen's (2003: 36) study on inter-ethnic relations reveals that among the five emerging paradigms in his study, the first paradigm—Traditional Eurocentric Racism—embraced a *white* American model that accepted all *white* Europeans of the Christian faith into the 'national fold' and accepted them as Americans, except for the Jews whose non-Christian religious affiliation kept them at a distance. Nevertheless, they too were regarded as part of the *white* American culture. On the other hand, non-Europeans—Blacks, American Indians (indigenous people), Asians and Mexicans—were 'considered inferior peoples, culturally and intellectually'.

Canada, Australia, South Africa and Britain also had a 'whites only' policy as part of their national citizenry goal. For instance, cultural and racial discrimination was legislated in South Africa from 1948–94. This was a form of institutional racism built into social structures such as the government and schools so that it allowed systematic exploitation and oppression of Black, Coloured and Indian people. South African cultural and racial relations were dominated by the legislated policy of Apartheid during this period and it was used to keep non-white groups segregated from the White population. 'Apartheid means separateness... and, as of 1948, it was the official policy of the South African government' (Denneburg, 1991: 30). Under Apartheid legislation, the Whites also enjoyed the privileges granted to them by the national state on the basis of their white skin colour while Black, Indian and Coloured people were regarded in the same inferior manner as described by Janzen (2003). Apartheid was practiced in South Africa until 1994 when President Nelson Mandela was elected the first African President of the country making South Africa a new democracy. According to Suderman (2007), in Australia, the 'whites only' policy was only completely abolished as late as 1975 when the Racial Discrimination Act was introduced, and in Canada it happened in 1971 when Canada adopted multiculturalism and began a concerted effort to attract immigrants. The Race Relations Act was recently flouted by the British National Party which is advocating a whites-only membership policy. According to a BBC online media report, 'The British National Party has been warned it has one last chance to scrap its whites-only membership policy or face a possible court injunction' (BBC website, January 2010).

## Cultural and Racial Discrimination

Cultural and racial discrimination may occur simultaneously during any intercultural communication encounter. When people from different cultural groups interact or communicate about socio-political, economic or education issues, they bring with them culture-specific understandings, attitudes and behaviours. They speak from their cultural knowledge and they interpret the communication from their cultural perspective more specifically than their general or limited knowledge of the target culture. Gudykunst and Kim (1997) describe the example of a business person from the United States conducting a transaction in an Arab setting. In this scenario, the United States representative may cross his or her legs during the meeting and this posturing or body language will be interpreted as an insult by the Arab person. The Arab will interpret this from his or her own cultural perspective, whereas the United States representative who did not intend to insult the Arab has little or no knowledge about the Arab culture. The inadequate knowledge of the Arab culture creates intercultural communication tension. Furthermore, Roberts, Davies and Jupp (1992) claim that persons from different cultures employ their cultural communication styles in the course of their interaction and use a different set of linguistic cues to get their meaning across. They further state that different speech communities have different communicative conventions. In this regard, Madhubuthi (1990) affirms that people view themselves and operate in the world through a consciousness which is influenced by their culture.

When people from different cultural groups are excluded or disadvantaged in any way, the result is discrimination. Gudykunst and Kim (1997) state that discrimination involves behaving in such a way that members of an 'out-group' are treated disadvantageously. When race and culture are identified as factors to exclude and treat certain groups differently, then racial and cultural discrimination might gravely disadvantage members of these groups considerably, especially in a workplace situation. Racially and culturally profiled groups might be ostracized and isolated deliberately and in subtle ways.

The study by Gumperz, Jupp and Roberts (1979) entitled 'Crosstalk', analysed the cultural and racial tensions between native English speaking people in England and the Asian and Afro-Caribbean communities whom they encountered in the work situation. This study and the racially segregated legislated government policy in South Africa between 1948 and 1994 are two examples of how cultural and racial discrimination was effectively accomplished. In the 'Crosstalk' study, the researchers identified three main reasons for the misunderstandings and miscommunications that arise when people from different ethnic groups or cultures interact in routine situations, such as in a job interview or asking for assistance in the bank. These are as follows:

1. Different cultural assumptions about the situation and about appropriate behaviour and intentions within it;
2. different ways of structuring information or an argument in a conversation; and
3. different ways of speaking—the use of a different set of unconscious linguistic conventions (such as tone of voice) to emphasize, to signal connections and logic, and to imply the significance of what is being said in terms of overall meaning and attitudes.

These research findings present evidence of the fact that inadequate cultural knowledge on the part of the second language speaker and the native speaker together contribute to the miscommunication across cultures. It is not sufficient for the second language speaker simply to have knowledge of linguistic use or fluency in the target language—which in this instance was English. In fact, the Gumperz, Jupp and Roberts' study used second language speakers who were fluent speakers of the language. In other words, they began with the assumption that fluency in the English language would help to ease problems of miscommunication. They admit that such a view presupposes that the acquisition of a basic level of English, on its own, will enable Asians—according to their study—to become effective communicators with other ethnic groups. One of their findings during the course of their study was that basic knowledge of the English language was not adequate for effective intercultural communication. They discarded this assumption as too simplistic and then identified other factors which acted discriminately against a person during an intercultural encounter such as:

1. Lack of knowledge of the cultural assumptions of Asians by non-Asians (usually the English people).
2. Lack of knowledge of the difficulties of speakers of English as a second language.

Both of the aforementioned factors have the potential to obstruct intercultural communication or to affect it negatively.

For effective communication between groups of people, each of the groups will have to acquire, learn or have adequate knowledge about each other's cultures before they begin to draw conclusions about each other's beliefs, attitudes and behaviours in a particular situation. The 'Crosstalk' study highlights another grave assumption made by the researchers and by the English group of people in their project. This assumption was the belief that only the second language speaker (the Asian) was responsible for the miscommunicated messages and had the responsibility of knowing about the target language culture. This view, therefore, absolves the English group or the first language speakers of their role in the communication process and excuses them of any responsibility of knowing about the Asian culture. It is evident from this scenario that since communication is an interaction between two or more people it cannot be the responsibility of only one of the individuals involved in the interaction to know the language and culture of the other. Otherwise, there would seem to be some degree of discrimination and unequal status already embedded in this approach.

Roberts, Davies and Jupp (1992) also state that language is a hidden dimension within discrimination and that it is used as a powerful tool to exert control. They contend that language is not often seen by most people as a factor within a discriminatory process. The South African case is a prime example of how the Afrikaans language was used as such a tool to exert control and to deny access. Obviously, those who do not see language as a discriminatory factor are those who are oblivious of the use of language as a manipulative tool within the greater political framework of any country and in a global context. The hegemony of English, for example, is often contested, but it retains its control and dominance as the language of the global workplace.

For second language speakers, proficiency in the second language is a means of survival. It means that they can compete for better jobs that guarantee a better life. Second language speakers feel the pressure, the tensions and the stress of learning the language and of using it in a culturally acceptable way. In a country like South Africa, language is associated with oppression and deprivation. The Afrikaans language, which was the language of the minority Nationalist government was imposed on all the citizens of the country. The use of language here as a manipulative tool to control access to education opportunities and jobs is of special significance in the South African context. People had to learn the language if one wanted access to better jobs even though the language was viewed as an instrument of oppression. The oppressive weight of the Nationalist government policy was felt even more sharply because the access to better jobs was further blocked along racial lines. Government policy favoured job reservations for the white minority population at nearly all job levels except for menial tasks. Even today, in a global context, the English language remains the access tool to better jobs and opportunities in Canada, Australia, the USA and Britain. Suderman (2007) highlights the case of Oscar Diaz whose language difficulties kept him in jobs that did not meet his professional needs and working at several jobs did not give him time for language classes. In the South African case, language proficiency and racial classification were used as criteria to deny job opportunities.

Gumperz, Jupp and Roberts (1979) point to some of the areas of 'cultural irritation' which was experienced by both the English and Asian groups in their study.

'Cultural irritation' refers to the annoyance a person from one culture feels and visibly displays when interacting with persons from another culture. This may take the form of a visible display of impatience, intolerance or frowning while the person from the opposite culture is speaking. One of the more significant aspects of 'cultural irritation' was noted in the styles of communication adopted by both groups of people. The Asian participants used the indirect style of speech when responding to questions while the English group expected the direct style of responses since this is their style of speech in all communications. The English group was annoyed, impatient and intolerant as the Asian attempted to explain their answers to the questions posed. Gudykunst (1991) states that the area of directness of speech used is another aspect of communication that often leads to miscommunication between high-and-low-context cultures which is further discussed under diverse communication styles.

It is interesting to note from the research by Gumperz, Jupp and Roberts (1979) that in Britain, the South Asian and Afro-Caribbean groups saw English as the language of power and status and as their 'access' to better jobs but soon realized that racism and discrimination operated equally strongly on the job market even though they spoke the language. In this study, one South Asian participant remarked he felt that once people saw his face they already made assumptions and that they did not listen to what he had to say. In the same study, it was evident that English language proficiency of the South Asian and Afro-Caribbean did not ease the intercultural interaction. Some degree of racial discrimination affected the intercultural interactions. In other words, although the participant spoke English fluently, it was the participant's cultural speech patterns along with the colour of his or her eyes, hair and skin which obstructed the intercultural communication process. This lends credence to the conclusion by Lustig and Koester (1996) that racial factors can be a major obstacle to intercultural communication.

## Current Trends in the Global Workplace

Current trends such as new media, air transportation and population shifts have impacted the global workplace, thereby posing intercultural communication challenges. More particularly, technological advancements such as higher levels of broadband and faster access to the Internet create endless possibilities for swifter communication and information dissemination in a broader world context. For example, Google in China has grown into a multi-billion dollar investment in a short space of time and the advent of the World Wide Web has also brought new challenges on the political front. Further, innovations such as blogs, twitter, podcasts and youtube technology have added to the speed of information travelling in a myriad of global virtual networks crossing news and views in an asynchronous timeframe transcending spatial and temporal boundaries.

At another level, air transportation has revolutionized travel times and mobility of populations making it easier to move between continents, into and out of workplace environments without a great deal of angst and travel time being lost. These developments have aided the unstable global economy in North America and other parts of the world, shaking markets out of their stupor and into new business options. Today, the reality of 'business beyond borders' in terms of global outsourcing, acquisitions, mergers and alliances have all transformed the way business was usually done for decades. In addition, trade agreements (NAFTA, FTAA, GATT, EU, CSME) provide a diverse range of opportunities for millions of people. These revolutionary changes have rendered the global workplace as the proverbial 'salad bowl', 'melting pot' or 'tossed salad'.

Current trends in population shifts suggest that *push* and *pull* factors in the global economy directly and indirectly influence the degree of global workforce mobility. *Push* factors such as wars, poverty, natural disasters and ethnic conflicts force people to uproot and seek other more secure places to live, study and work. On the other hand, *pull* factors such as better quality of education, job opportunities, peace and prosperity bring people of different cultures, religious and political persuasions into the same global workplace arena. Following disappointment in their governments and fear of brutality, many bring with them their dreams of a better future and their hopes for their children. They also bring with them their cultural, ethnic and racial baggage, inevitably creating a potentially and realistically explosive situation. In other words, as a result of *push* and *pull* factors, immigrants, refugees and migrants often become embroiled in racial and ethnic clashes with members of the national populations to which they migrate. Suderman (2007: 22) claims that 'conflict over immigration and cultural pluralism has begun to unsettle countries like The Netherlands, Britain and France'. Some of these conflicts remain confined to the workplace, often in the silent office corridors, when multiple cultures come together, each with their unique worldviews, perceptions, expectations and communication quirks. Other conflicts spill onto the streets and in the neighbourhoods. The recent conflict between the Rumanians and the Irish in Ireland; the

South Asian muggings and murders in Melbourne, Australia; and the Islamaphobia media reports from Switzerland, Germany and France are some examples. These upheavals lend credence to Lustig and Koester's (2006: 155) assertion, for example, that 'immigrants to the United States have not always been accepted into the communities into which they have settled'.

## Diversity in Communication Styles

O'Hair, Friedrich and Dixon (2008: 131) contend that since 'language varies in its preciseness', it is important to explore new ways of expressing what you mean. In this regard, it is important to consider the *environment* in which the message is sent and received, the nature of the *communication* being sent and particularly, the *expectations* of the sender and receiver. In other words, consideration of the environment, communication and the expectation would ensure that the message is appropriately constructed and conveyed in an appropriate manner and that any misunderstanding of the communication would be reviewed in relation to external influences during the conveyance of the message while also giving special consideration of differing expectations of the sender and receiver.

Factors that complicate the message include culture, race, gender and age and each demands appropriate responses and gestures. Among the classic research framework from which intercultural communication researchers have borrowed for decades, is the high-and-low-context cultural taxonomy of Hall (1976). He categorizes the exchanged messages which take place during any intercultural experience as high-and-low-context cultures. High-context (HC) cultures are culturally homogeneous and messages are usually conveyed on the understanding that there is a long-term relationship and degree of mutual understanding and respect among all parties. The Japanese, Chinese, South Korean, African, Native American and Arab cultures have been identified as high-context cultures. In low-context (LC) cultures, there is greater diversity among members of the culture. Members of this culture are also known to disagree and often rely on formal written contracts and agreements. The American, French, English and German cultures are among those identified with low-context cultures. HC and LC messages and cultural characteristics may give us some indication of how these high-and-low-context cultures communicate and interact in the global workplace. However, as noted earlier, as a result of an increasing mobility of individuals and groups, as well as a higher trend of assimilation of minority cultures around the world, we must acknowledge that it is possible that not all high-and-low-context cultures behave in the same way in the twenty-first century.

While contexts may vary, it is the *meaning* of the communication that is of paramount importance in any intercultural encounter. To this end, it is necessary to contextualize a communication event or to place it in context, if one wants to make meaning of it. Hall (1976) contends that meaning and context are inextricably bound with each other. The messages exchanged between people have been categorized by him into HC and LC messages. Accordingly, he makes the following claim:

> A high-context (HC) communication or message is one in which most of the information is either in the physical context or internalized in the person, while very little is in the coded, explicit, transmitted part of the message. A low-context (LC) communication is just the opposite i.e. the mass of information is vested in the explicit code. (Ibid.: 91)

Gudykunst (1991) adds that the area of directness of speech used is an area where misunderstandings and miscommunication may occur between low-and high-context cultures. LC cultures use direct styles of speech while HC cultures use indirect styles of speech. However, it is worth noting that neither Hall (1976) nor Gudykunst and Kim (1997) explain that while national cultures such as that of the United States of America or England may be regarded as LC cultures, one cannot ignore the fact that many subcultures exist within these national cultures and that these subcultures are not necessarily LC cultures. There may be differing degrees of HC and LC cultures within a single national culture.

Gudykunst (1991) defines LC cultures as those with direct styles of speech while members of HC cultures use indirect styles of speech. LC cultures such as the United States of America and Britain are also regarded as individualistic cultures since they emphasize the 'I' in direct speech and usually offer short, direct responses. In the high-context cultures, also regarded as collectivistic cultures, such as India, Greece and Japan, the member of the collectivist culture uses 'we' even to express a personal viewpoint. Members of this culture may offer broad generalizations and begin with seemingly 'irrelevant' information in their responses.

Evidently, the mode of verbal and non-verbal communication among racially and culturally diverse individuals and groups is fraught with cultural and racial baggage. Consequently, current organizational frameworks have implemented mechanisms to respond to racial and cultural diversity in the workplace through established and recognized diversity programmes, affirmative action protocols and equal opportunity offices. However, even with the presence of these mechanisms in a number of organizations around the world, the language of workplace communication is still unable to shed its biased and discriminatory flavour.

## Barriers to Intercultural Communication

The multifaceted nature of culture undoubtedly impacts the already complex behaviour of human beings which invariably results in a range of communication challenges or barriers. This problem is particularly evident in communication between and among people of diverse cultural backgrounds. In other words, while there is a natural tendency to seek out people who are similar to us in terms of common features and cultural traits, this may not always be possible. Alternatively, intercultural encounters and accompanying challenges or barriers are inevitable. It is, therefore, important to be aware of these barriers and even more essential to learn how to manage them by developing some degree of intercultural competence. According to Lustig and Koester (1996), stereotyping or forming generalizations about groups of people, prejudice (negative attitudes towards people based on flawed and rigid stereotypes), discrimination (active prejudice evident by displaying certain behaviour) and racism (exclusion of certain people because of race) are four broad categories identified as obstacles to intercultural competence. Other barriers include ethnocentrism, intercultural phobia, language and the host country experience.

## Practice of Stereotyping

At a most basic level, stereotyping is the tendency to mentally categorize people into groups which in turn influence our behaviour towards them. Walter Lippman is credited for this description as a habit of organizing our observation of people into categories as representative of the larger grouping. This is a convenient strategy of simplifying our complex world into categories for easy reference and understanding. It is important to note, however, that stereotyping is not an innate trait but rather cultivated over a period of time and experiences. Consequently, these generalizations may not be accurate and are usually hastily formed based on limited or chance encounters. In this regard, we need to be wary of stereotypes perpetuated through the media, notably television and cinema which often succeed in promoting distorted or convenient versions of reality. The practice of stereotyping can also lead to the tendency to *label* others as belonging to categories. This negative connotation is also referred to as 'cultural labelling'.

## Role of Prejudicial Attitudes

While stereotyping is about putting people into categories, prejudice is a learned habit of forming fixed impressions or attitudes based on these generalizations. These attitudes or prejudices are targeted to a certain religion, gender, age, sexual orientation or social class. Negative attitudes or feeling often descend into hostility as in the case of profiling Muslims in the aftermath of 9/11 as potential terrorists or perceiving all Rastafarians as users of marijuana. In other words, prejudicial attitudes tend to reinforce a feeling of superiority and power in its practitioners. However, its practice varies from the overt to subtle behaviours. As a whole, these hostilities are perpetuated by dominant cultures against minority groups.

## Overt and Covert Forms of Racism

When the attitude of prejudice becomes more entrenched in our minds as a firm belief, we become prone to practising racism. Perpetrators of racism hold the view that their racial category is superior to others.

Today, racism remains one of the great scourges that continue to haunt humankind. In spite of the chorus of condemnation from noted global citizens such as Martin Luther King, Mahatma Gandhi, Nelson Mandela and Bishop Desmond Tutu among others, this social evil plagues almost every facet of our lives. In keeping with the advocacy of these fine minds, countries with plural societies such as South Africa, Mauritius, Fiji, Guyana and Trinidad and Tobago have established institutions that address problems of race as well as conduct related research. These initiatives would contribute towards enlightenment of those ignorant about race, as well as its associated problems such as stereotyping and prejudice. More importantly, so-called superior races would appreciate the value of tempering their intercultural interactions with ethical considerations and universal equality of treatment. In retrospect, it is important to recognize that we often fail to realize that the single most divisive element that drives us apart is not race, as we are inclined to think, but differences in culture.

## Forms of Workplace Discrimination

Whereas prejudice and racism are mental states in the forms of attitude and belief respectively, discrimination is the act of treating someone differently because of the person's racial or ethnic background, often from a minority group. Differences in gender, language and religion can also sow seeds of discrimination. Regardless of the context or environment, discrimination is morally wrong and contributes to tension and discomfort, whether it is practised subtly or visibly. Discrimination in the workplace, for example, can affect all parties involved such as employees, managers, messengers and customers. Cases of discrimination by elements of dominant cultures against minorities seeking employment are well documented, as indeed similar claims as regards salary, training, promotion and performance evaluations even when hired.

## Ethnocentric Perspectives

Ethnocentrism, the tendency by one group or culture to use its own culture to evaluate the actions of others, is an obstacle to intercultural competence. Suderman (2007: 35) suggests that 'ethnocentrism is a two-part assumption' that one's culture is better than the other culture and that people have a desire to be like one's own culture. This ethnocentric bias or tunnel-vision towards one's culture is also described as 'cultural myopia'. She points to various forms of ethnocentrism that include positive and negative notions and institutional, individual and national implementation of ethnocentrism. More commonly, however, we can be branded as ethnocentric if we view others cultures through the narrow lens of our own cultures. Given the plethora of cultures, it is not surprising that ethnocentrism is present in almost every culture whose members regard theirs as superior to other cultures. In spite of its negative connotation, however, it is important to note that ethnocentrism is not deliberate but acquired at the unconscious level, through curricula in schools, folktales through the oral tradition, and so on. In other words, ethnocentrism can be unwittingly institutionalized in a school system through religious studies promoting the teachings of a particular religion. The subtlety of ethnocentrism is evident in American classrooms that promote a worldview of American supremacy and standards to its students. At worst, ethnocentrism can lead to marginalization of co-cultures from the dominant culture that is present in today's workplace, school and the wider society. Whatever the form, it is important to recognize ethnocentrism and confront it in order to level the playing filed particularly in the context of today's increasingly diverse workplace.

## Intercultural Phobia

Intercultural communication encounters in recent years have given rise to a number of phobias or fears arising from actual or potential intercultural conflicts, based particularly on religious and territorial wars and events around the globe. Currently, most other phobias of the past century have been laid to rest and in its place we have an incredibly, strong emergence of Islamophobia—fear of Muslims and their religion, Islam. Islamophobia has gone beyond and above the September 11 (2001) attacks on the Twin Towers in NYC and has taken on a life of its own.

The Bollywood movie *My Name is Khan* depicts the post-9/11 paranoia and Islamaphobia brilliantly. Jenni Miller's (2010) review of the movie captures the highlights of the film and its success as a box office hit in the USA where it netted USD1.86 million. The film portrays the stereotypical and prejudiced behaviour of the American public in San Francisco after the 9/11 bombing of the Twin Towers in New York by 'Arab terrorists'. In the movie, Khan who is an Asperger's syndrome sufferer, makes it his mission to meet the President of the United States to tell him, 'My name is Khan and I am not a terrorist', after losing his step-son, Sameer to the post-9/11 racial riots and tensions. Ironically, the movie also renewed violence and tension between Hindus and Muslims in India when, according to a BBC report (2010), cinemas advertising the movie were vandalized and cinemagoers had to be protected. While Americans are coming to terms with the aftermath of that horrific event and are making amends to build a strong, diverse workforce, the British, Germans, Swiss, French, Swedish and Dutch have increased their attack on Islam and Muslims which range from banning buildings with minarets to placing a ban on head covers of Muslim women. These and other phobias can also be found in the workplace.

## Crossing the Language Divide

Another challenge to intercultural communication is language. This challenge is equally evident in the context of the workplace. Language is the tool of transferring messages and the objective is to establish shared meaning between parties. While language involves the use of both verbal and non-verbal codes, the meanings generated by each language are influenced by particular cultures. The differences among codes and symbols often defy the goal of a common understanding. Today, the multiplicity of languages globally and variations thereof undoubtedly contribute to intercultural challenges such as discrimination. Language is the least visible, least measurable and least understood aspects of discrimination (Roberts, Davies and Jupp, 1992). A case in point is the legislated policy of racial segregation and the displacement of ethnic or mother tongue languages during the apartheid years in South Africa.

## Host Country Experience

Immigrants to Canada and New Zealand, for example, find that their lack of host country work experience denies them access to jobs. Often, they are either excluded when their resumes are reviewed or rejected at the interview stage because they lack Canadian or New Zealand experience. Only recently, the Ontario Province Human Rights Commission announced that denying job applicants an opportunity to be hired on the basis of not having 'Canadian experience' would be regarded as a violation of their rights. In New Zealand, migrants are denied jobs on the basis of lack of New Zealand experience which Lewis (2009) found to be the case in her research among migrant women. She found that 'despite qualifications and experience in other parts of the world, migrants were often rejected because they lacked New Zealand experience' (Ibid.: 42).

# Enhancing Intercultural Communication

The foregoing barriers to intercultural communication which are commonplace in today's global workplace may, understandably, present a daunting picture. Nevertheless, members of the diverse workplace can employ any or a combination of techniques to overcome these barriers depending on the specific nature of the intercultural context. It is important to remember, however, that the suggestions offered here are not meant to be prescriptive. Each situation would first have to be objectively assessed according to one's own knowledge and experiences before addressing the challenge at hand. Eventually, one would succeed in honing one's skills in dealing with the myriad of multicultural encounters for the simple reason that, in the final analysis, one must take responsibility for one's actions. The following steps, though not exhaustive, require time, energy and commitment:

1. *Conduct a personal self-assessment*: It is important to begin with yourself. Assess your own attitudes towards other cultures and

co-cultures because they can influence your communication with these cultures. After all, what you bring to the communication event can very well determine the success or failure of that event. Ongoing self-analysis or introspection should involve the stages of knowing one's culture, knowing one's perception and knowing how to act on those perceptions.

2. *Consider the setting and context*: Setting and context can influence the outcome of our communication encounters. Timing, for example, is an important consideration in communication and varies with different cultures. We must acknowledge its importance and determine the most appropriate time to engage in business or pleasure with members of other cultures for best results.

3. *Open communication channels*: No one channel can guarantee successful communication. As the context, culture or person varies, we must be flexible or adjust our communication behaviour. Adaptability is therefore essential as each situation warrants. Competence in intercultural communication behoves us to develop a repertoire of skills, strategies, tactics or techniques to manage situations as they arise.

4. *Practice supportive communication*: One very supportive communication behaviour is empathy. Empathy allows us to imagine ourselves in the cultural world of others and try to experience what they experience. In this way, we allow ourselves to appreciate others and build tolerance for them.

5. *Develop language competencies* Language is the tool or medium of communication. However, language and its meanings vary with cultures and is *culture bound* or *culture specific*. Clichés and idioms, for example, must be avoided and focus should instead be on literal meaning in order to avoid confusion or misinterpretation. Learning the language of others can also be very beneficial and we stand to get a better sense of their variations and nuances. We also develop a sensitivity to the different codes in both the verbal and nonverbal language of other cultures.

6. *Encourage feedback*: Effective feedback is important in communication and even more crucial in intercultural encounters. Feedback verifies understanding or shared meaning and can be verbal or nonverbal as well as intentional or unintentional. Always strive to ensure that feedback is immediate, honest, specific, and clear. This eliminates confusion or misunderstanding. It is therefore important to invite or encourage feedback even if it takes the form of silent feedback.

7. *Develop appreciation toward diversity*: It is equally important to learn about other cultures and co-cultures. They are different and we stand to learn from them. In other words, diverse populations provide opportunities for learning. We must appreciate the richness of the differences we discover and learn to develop an appreciation for them. View diversity as an opportunity to learn and enhance our intercultural competencies.

8. *Avoid stereotypes*: As mentioned previously, stereotypes are broad generalizations or categories that can often be misleading. We must refrain from the tendency to treat others based on these assumptions. Instead, we must make conscious attempts to know members of other cultures individually and treat them accordingly. Appreciate each person for who he or she is and respect the worth of each individual.

9. *Avoid ethnocentrism*: There is an inherent bias in lauding your culture and ethnicity as the best. This may only be true in your setting or context and based on your familiarity. However, this so-called superiority may be challenged when you're exposed to other cultures that can show shortcomings in your own culture. It is, therefore, advisable, to be open-minded and appreciate the lessons of other cultures while still valuing your own.

10. *Develop a sense of universalism*: Our intercultural or diverse world is characterized by a multitude of differences. It is important to move from a state of myopia and foster a sense of universalism. In other words, always strive for the common ground that would seek to unite us as global citizens irrespective of differences in culture, race, ethnicity, gender, class, sexual orientation and physical challenges.

# Conclusion

It is evident from the foregoing discussion that we are still not any closer in meeting Hall's (1976) challenge which he posed nearly two decades ago: 'Man must now embark on the difficult journey beyond culture, because the greatest separation feat of all is when one manages to gradually free oneself from the grip of unconscious culture' (Ibid.: 240). Some of the questions arising from this discussion are in what way has the notion of intercultural communication moved away from an 'us (dominant culture) and them' paradigm; what measures have been implemented to monitor a fair and respectful workplace; and how have these measures created a harmonious diversity. It is hoped that the information provided in this chapter will help provide answers to these questions. As one reflects on them, one can think about how to hone one's own intercultural communication competencies to help improve harmony and enhance productivity in the workplace.

# Chapter 7

# Cultural Perceptions on Environment and Global Contexts

Jainism: 'A man should wander about treating all creatures as he himself would be treated.' *Sutrakritanga, 1.11.33*

## Introduction

Intercultural communication is deeply embedded in the values and belief systems of diverse cultures. Values and beliefs frame the way in which one's environment is perceived—acceptable and unacceptable norms of behaviour in a specific environment are conceived of as well as the manner in which communication is sent and received.

Environmental factors affect the way people send, receive, interpret and respond to messages. The perceptions of various cultures of their environment depend on their worldviews. Worldviews or the way an individual or group views the world around them impact directly on the relationships that they have with their environment and on the way in which their environment affects their communication. In this chapter, the relationship between culture, environment and worldviews is examined to determine how intercultural communication is affected by environmental perceptions. The role of factors such as time and distance are also reviewed to illustrate that these factors contribute to the complexity of intercultural communication.

The impact of environmental context is underestimated in intercultural communication. People are sometimes baffled at what went wrong during a specific communication interaction and do not consider the effects of the environment on communication. Often, the influence of the environment on the communication interaction goes unnoted and unrecognized as a significant factor that affects the success or failure of communication. Neuliep (2006: 25) presents a contextual model of intercultural communication that explains the effects of context on interpersonal interactions with each other across cultures. The contextual model illustrates the various contexts within which intercultural communication operates. Verbal and non-verbal messages filter through several layers of understanding moving from the perceptual context of the person from Culture A and from Culture B who may also have in common (or not) a socio-relational context. Other contexts through which the messages flow include the environmental context, micro-cultural context and the cultural context. This means that messages received and sent between the person from Culture A and from the person from Culture B have to be coded and decoded across the different contexts in order to be understood. Often, the influence of the environmental context is either not consciously noted or recognized by those participating in the intercultural communication encounter.

## What Do We Mean by Environment?

Environment refers to a number of different things and consists of several components. For example, Knapp and Hall (2006: 109) claim that environment refers to the natural spaces around us and includes the geographical space, the atmospheric condition and the location. Further, it also includes the architectural and design features such as shape, colour, structure, design, layout and movable objects, and it also refers to the presence and absence of other people. It is for this reason that any type of communication is said to be affected by its environment. When people communicate across cultures, the perceptions of their immediate environment and, as Neuliep (2006) suggests, both their perceptual contexts and their socio-relational contexts affect their communication.

Other factors that affect the messages received and sent in any environmental context include the information available within the environment context. For example, access to information is an important consideration as well as the volume, level and load of information being perceived and contained in that environment. These factors feature significantly in the way that communication is sent and received. The information rate or the volume of information contained or perceived in a unit of time affects how it will need to be processed. For example, the more information one receives or the higher rate of information— information overload—the longer it takes to process. A high information load refers to a situation in which there is a high information rate that includes information that is uncertain, complex and dense and a low information load refers to a situation where information is certain, simple and spare (Huber, O'Connell and Cummings, 1975). Information load is equivalent to the level of anxiety in an environment and the more familiar we are with an environment the less uncertainty and anxiety we experience. Of all environmental factors, people are the greatest source of uncertainty. When we interact with people from a range of diverse cultures, especially in their environment, then the information load is high.

Environments also affect our emotional reactions, according to Knapp and Hall (2006: 107). They contend that environments influence our level of stimulation, satisfaction and comfort. Environments contribute to how excited we are and how alert or active we become emotionally and they also affect our satisfaction and joyful emotional state. More importantly, environments create a comfortable or uncomfortable state, where the former is one in which we are either in control and are able to interact in a dominant way because we feel a sense of freedom to behave as we wish or in a way that is natural to us. Again, an environment with a lower information load provides a more supportive and positive experience, while an environment with a higher information load creates a high degree of anxiety with more negative perceptions and behaviour.

# Relationship between Culture, Environment and Worldviews

Suderman (2007: 154) claims that worldview in conjunction with territoriality is often at the core of conflict. A culture's worldview contextualizes the importance of their environment and that becomes the key basis upon which they construct their intercultural relationships. Diverse cultures value natural environments in different ways. The fact that a culture's relationship with nature is culture-bound means that cultural perspectives are deeply embedded in how cultural groups view nature. A culture's orientation toward nature determines how people within that culture communicate about nature and how they organize their daily activities around nature. Often, physical and climatic aspects of nature may restrict the kinds of activities that occur.

It is important to be cognizant of cultural perceptions and worldviews of the natural environment in order to be interculturally competent in a global context. Different cultures see the physical environment in different ways and seek different approaches to managing and solving their daily problems (Nunez, Madhi and Popma, 2007). Altman and Chemers (1984) categorize three different cultural orientations to nature:

1. *People as subjugated to nature*, living a life at the mercy of an uncontrollable force.
2. *People as over nature*, with a strong belief that people can dominate, exploit and control nature.
3. *People as an inherent part of nature*, where humans, animals, plants and other elements can live in harmony in an inter-dependent way.

These three orientations are effective ways of surviving and are important assumptions about people–environment relationship; one is not better than the other (Nunez, Mahdi and Popma, 2007). Cultural and societal dynamics suggest that even within a society or culture, there are people who hold one or two or a combination of the three orientations, all depending on situations and environmental factors.

In societies that are subjugated to nature, people believe that as their fate and destiny are dominated by the invisible power of nature, and so they completely accept the situation. In these societies, almost all physical objects and events are perceived to have life and power over their destiny. Whitfield (2004) maintains that people in such societies, Indonesia for example, tend to be superstitious, are unwilling to take responsibility for their own actions or to try hard to influence outcomes and change their fate. They are resigned to a belief that religion is the only way to help them out of the situation and do not wish to take initiative and personal will to exert effort to change one's life for the better. As a result, 'a quiet suffering is normally the proper response to life's problems'. They should be happy with their own life which is offered to them by God, nature and the universe. For generations, they believe in what they have been told by their ancestors. They follow village rituals, tradition, ceremonies, pray to the local spirits and objects of power and make sacrifices to them. It is their belief that if their rituals are not properly performed, God, nature and the universe will take serious retribution on the lives of those involved. Such duties are considered more important than work in the workplace. Even when mistreated in the workplace, they tend to accept this without making a fuss, because any expressive and direct response would clash with their belief that people who openly express their feelings and emotions are the ones who have been possessed by evil spirits. Therefore, loss of emotional control is frowned upon and is strongly discouraged.

Similar cultural orientations can also be found in the traditional rituals and ceremony of the Pumi ethnicity in Yunnan Province, China. The ancestor worshipping Pumi people worship nature, which they believe are responsible for the success or failure, happiness or tragedy of their life. On many occasions, such as celebrations, anniversaries, weddings, births, harvests and travel, prayers and sacrifices have to be made to an invisible power existing in a rock, a tree, the top of a mountain and a river, through a shaman to invite peace and dispel misfortune. The kitchen spirit is believed to take charge of the family's fortune and therefore respect for it is a priority in the family. They worship their ancestors and hold many rituals because they believe that the souls and spirits of their ancestors always survive, residing in their natal places or in the heaven. Rituals are also held and sacrifices made to invoke God to address the problems and provide peace when disharmony, quarrels, ailments and misfortunes occur in the family.

A culture's views about their natural environment also affects how they perceive and design their *built environment*. For example, cultural communities adapt their built environments to their worldviews of nature and this is visible in how they design the landscape, the lighting and the architecture of their dwellings. Aside from the economic and political considerations in designing buildings to meet their specific needs, cultural values and motivations play a significant role in the design of their abodes. While exterior designs take into consideration the landscape and other natural space issues, interiors are built to satisfy cultural values and beliefs about family, privacy, gender roles, social interaction and religious practices. The cultural perceptions about environments and interactions among individuals and groups within those affect intercultural communication in various ways.

Knapp and Hall (2006: 129) suggest that there are six perceptual bases for examining environments:

1. *Formal versus informal:* Formal and informal structures of the business establishments, offices, atmosphere and power relationships may increase or reduce the amount of social interaction.
2. *Warm versus cold:* A warm environment encourages interaction, such as warm greetings, smiles, offering of a cup of tea or an encouraging tone. A cold environment discourages interaction, such as seating arrangements at McDonalds are designed to encourage people to leave, not to linger.
3. *Private versus public:* A private environment is conducive to a more personal conversation than a public environment where impersonal conversation and public information are encouraged.
4. *Familiar versus unfamiliar:* The level of familiarity can reduce or increase people's anxiety and discomfort.
5. *Constraining versus free:* We may feel powerless and anxious when we realize that we have no control over the environment,

but we can feel psychologically comfortable when we find we have control over the environment.

6. *Distant versus close:* Physical, social and psychological distance may increase or discourage conversation and interaction.

All of the above environmental factors affect intercultural communication in varying degrees. Hall (1969) identifies four distance zone, appropriate for different types of communication and interaction (see, Griffin, 2009: 62–63):

1. Intimate distance 0–18 inches (for embracing, touching or whispering).
2. Personal distance 1.5–4 feet (for interaction among good friends).
3. Social distance 4–12 feet (for impersonal transaction and interaction among acquaintances).
4. Public distance over 12+ feet (set around important public figures for public speaking).

In the same way that distance affects intercultural communication, so does time. Time orientation or the perception and use of time is cultural. Hall's (1976) theory on time orientation across cultures is wellknown in intercultural communication. Hall's (Ibid.) M-Time or monochromic cultures and P-Time or polychromic cultures have been cited in intercultural communication literature exhaustively, suggesting that cultures function either in linear and orderly manner, doing one thing at a time or in a more flexible mode doing several things at the same time. Suderman (2007: 195) claims that North America and Northern Europe are M-Time cultures and Latin America, Africa and South Asia are regarded as P-Time cultures. We may want to consider the implications and complexities of intercultural communication in a global context when people from an M-Time cultural context move to a P-Time cultural context and vice versa.

Intercultural communication is complicated by the various environmental factors that affect the manner in which communication is sent and received. Factors such as structure, power relationships, distance and time play a role in the effectiveness of communication. Cultural worldviews and perspectives add further dimensions to the communication encounter.

# Conclusion

Cultural perceptions of environment affect intercultural communication encounters and interactions in a number of ways as illustrated in this discussion. The diversity of cultures and cultural worldviews in a global context certainly contribute to a more complex cultural dynamics on a global level.

It is important to consider the multiple complexities of intercultural communication in a global context before drawing conclusions about the success and/or failure of any intercultural communication interaction.

Chapter 8

# Technology as Cultural Power and Its Social Impact

Taoism: 'Regard your neighbour's gain as your own gain and your neighbour's loss as your own loss. *T'ai Shang Kan Ying P'ien*

## Introduction

Technology in various forms, from television and radio to digital technologies like the Internet and email, is a culturally powerful force that impacts intercultural interactions in a myriad ways. Bonilla and Cliche (2004) claim that the social impact of the Internet is significant and they claim that the Internet, for example, intensifies the inequities in society. Research studies (Rogers, 1995; Levine and Donitsa-Schmidt, 1998; Rao, 1997) into the degree of influence and impact of technology on human relations spans a wide range of issues such as the uses, attitudes and effects of media among diverse (for e.g., in terms of socio-economic status, power differentials, age and gender) populations in general, and the impact of technology on social and intercultural interactions, in particular. In the 1980s and 1990s, much of the literature (Mowlana, 1995; Williams, Rice and Rogers, 1988; Wilkins, 1999) focused on access to and gender relationships in online communication through the Internet and email. The social impact of technology and the recognition of technology as culture had also been advocated by McLuhan and Pacey in the 1960s to 1980s; and it has resurfaced today as a significant phenomenon in the twenty-first century because of the wide-ranging influence of technology and the multiple forms of technology (from the Internet and email to the iPhone and iPad).

McLuhan (1962) is regarded as a pioneer and visionary in terms of his deep insights into the social influence of media and the depth of impact of technology advancement on human communication around the globe in the future. McLuhan suggested that technology would minimize time and distance in ways that would reduce the world into a 'global village'. McLuhan also predicted a phenomenal role for technology in the future and today information and communication technologies (ICTs) are rapidly surpassing the role of traditional communication media at any given time in the past century. The Internet and email, for instance, are an asynchronous media that transcend time and distance allowing people to communicate around the globe 24/7. Mass communication literature (Lerner, 1958; Rogers, 1962; McMichael, 2004) has identified ways in which technology has created favourable conditions to advance and positively influence communication around the world. In some instances, the literature (McMichael, 2004) suggests that while the advent of technology brought with it the promise of advancement and prosperity for developing and developed nations alike, the reality is less glorified. Communities around the world continue to experience gross economic hardship, financial disasters and human suffering in spite of technological advancement and because of it. According to Gurumurthy (2004: 7), the 'dramatic positive changes' heralded by ICTs have not 'touched all of humanity'.

On the one hand, many findings and recommendations have emerged to inform us of the negative impact of technology on human communication, whereas on the other hand, myths about the positive impact of technology abound. Underlying these myths are particularly naive notions that intercultural communication in cyberspace discards stereotypical behaviours and that technology is free of value and culture bias. Particularly noteworthy is the decades old notion that technology is neutral and Pacey (1983: 5) disputes this myth and claims that technology is not 'value-fee and politically neutral'. Gurumurthy (2004: 7) claims that since 'power relations in society determine the enjoyment of benefits from ICTs; hence these technologies are not gender neutral'.

She strongly advocates a gendered approach in which technology and culture are intricately entwined and also recognizes the overwhelming social impact of technology. The research trends in the next century have established that ICTs not only influence the culture of gendered relations online, but that ICTs are in themselves a culture. Palomba (2006: 83) supports this line of argument and suggests that 'cyberspace itself has a culture and is not culture-free'. However, Palomba also asserts that technology is 'simply a neutral and value-free platform for exchange'. As a platform, technology offers various advantages like a sense of security and confidence, empowerment, achievement, and a space to exchange views and opinions, anonymity, and so on, to users, who rely on it as their information and communication tool.

Research evidence related to technological enhancement of communication suggests ways in which technological communication made is better, different and more accessible. While this may be true in some instances, as noted by Gurumurthy (2006: 3) as it includes strategies that empower women, amplify their voices, educate women on their rights, build capacity and networking potential, technology may not always have positive impact. Palomba (2006) claims that there are various myths regarding the positive impact of intercultural communication on cyberculture. Among the vast research in this area are studies that support claims that ICTs promote intercultural learning; develop positive attitudes and an appreciation of the perspectives of 'other' cultures; ICTs are value-free and that they help to overcome deep social and cultural divisions. Silva (2004) claims that the economic benefits of ICTs and the development of technological infrastructure have been exaggerated without consideration 'of the social and cultural impact of these technologies'. The inequities created by the ICTs such as the Internet has also been noted by Bonilla and Cliche (2004) who contend that it has led to a redistribution of material and cultural wealth which has also resulted in the reproduction of 'the dominant order, based on social exclusion and on racial, ethnic, gender or generational inequality'. Gurumurthy (2010) is of the view that 'the marginalities crafted by the information society pursues gendered hierarchies, creating, first of all, the primary faultline separating those with access to and membership in digital spaces and information networks and those without'. Further, she claims that issues of inequity, disadvantage and marginality resulting from so called technological advancement are underplayed in the broader global context of *political economic correctness* because those who profit from the technological investments that fill their pockets, aspire to higher levels of privilege and advantage. For technology investors, the key to their success lies in marketing the pivotal role of information and communication technologies (ICTs) such as the Internet, email and mobile telephone to improve and advance human communication. Advertising companies and technology product manufacturers rarely publicize the negative, harmful effects of the ICTs on the health, environment and socio-economic status of users. Technology as cultural power and its social impact is a young field of research and requires greater advocacy and recognition at national and global level.

This chapter subscribes to the notion *of technology as culture* suggesting that technology is embedded in a socio-cultural framework that affects the political economy status of communities and impacts on human relations in various ways. Furthermore, technology *as cultural power* is acknowledged as one of the significant mechanisms responsible for widening the digital, socio-economic, innovation and gender-divide at an alarming rate. Finally, discussion in the chapter focuses on ways in which technology impacts on social interactions creating another complex layer of human communication locked between the virtual and the real world. Simply borrowing and switching skills and strategies between the two worlds, making assumptions about technology's grand elasticity to contain the multiple faces of humanness and engaging online users in simulated and augmented realities is not adequate to meet the complexities of online communication. Particularly, it is important to recognize that technology as cultural power impacts all forms of interactions in ways that lie beyond our imagination.

In order to understand technology's cultural power, it is necessary to recognize technology as culture and situate it within the literature as a dynamic catalyst that controls patterns of technology-user behaviour and that drives technological innovation and change. An exploration of the literature on technology and culture reveals that scholars and researchers approach the technology and culture relationship in diverse ways. In discussions (Tannen, 1996; Kantrowitz, 1996; Harraway, 1996) on technology as gendered culture (women and men's cultural behaviour online) and online gender wars (claims over virtual territory), claims abound that women and men carry their gender baggage online and behave in ways that they do in the real world. Kantrowitz (1996: 134) claimed that 'computer culture is created, defined and controlled by men'. Harraway (1996: 146) claimed that women and men adopt gendered styles online. It is seen that the male-gendered style is assertive, self-promoting, sarcastic, authoritative and self-confident while female-gendered styles display a more supportive, polite, clarifying, less-confrontational online behaviour. Another characteristic typical of male-oriented behaviour that is common in online communication is referred to as the 'flame wars', which We (1993) described as the posting of angry responses by male online users. Technology as culture is contextualized through acceptable and unacceptable norms and behaviours, with women in subordinate roles attempting to negotiate and men in dominant roles claiming virtual space as their territory. The contextual association defines technology as power, giving the users of that technology greater or lesser significance depending on their power differentials, gendered hierarchies, the sophistication of the technology being used, ease of access (or not) to that technology, the user's socio-economic status and how technologically savvy the user is in terms of the software, hardware and the technical language. Technology is also approached as a phenomenon that either influences culture or that is in turn influenced by diverse cultures.

In subscribing to technology as culture, we accept that technology affects human behaviour in the same way that diverse cultures (for e.g., popular culture, national culture, ethnic culture, research culture and consumer culture) affect human behaviour.

## Subscribing to Technology as Culture

Technology as a culture assumes power and privilege in the same way as other cultures do. Paz (2004) is of the view that the Internet, is a 'cultural phenomenon' and that it 'is clearly much more than a technological object; it represents a cultural shift that affects all the dimensions of a community, a group or a society'. There is an increasing consciousness noted in recent research to recognize the cultural role of technology and its social impact. It has moved beyond the early years of technology research that was framed around the gender gap in online communication, the norms and protocols of online behaviours, and the digital divide among the wealthy and the poor. Pacey (1983: 2) introduced the notion of the culture of technology in the early 1980s when he refuted the old argument that technology 'is culturally, morally and politically neutral'. According to him, those who operate at different levels of power are enabled because of their ability to exploit and manipulate 'deeper values relating to the so-called technological imperative, and to the basic creativity that makes innovation possible' (Ibid.: 12). Thus, he argues that the power to exploit values is a central thesis of the culture of technology.

## Technology as Cultural Power

Technology as a culture and as cultural power may be recognized by the attributes that become aligned and associated with technology since its inception. The unique language spoken by technocrats becomes a language of power, excluding those who do not understand it and including those who do. The introduction of techno-dialects around the world is another growing characteristic of embracing technology as cultural power. Techno-dialects refer to the embedding of techno-cultural language within the native languages and remote geographical regions around the world so that indigenous communities can navigate their virtual worlds and thereby control their destinies. Guatemalans learning to use computers through 'computer software in their native Mayan language, Ki'che' (Guenette and Beamish, 2005) is a good case in point that illustrates how the cultural power of technology is infused with the language and culture of a rural and indigenous society. The Enlache Quiche non-governmental project aimed at 'building a virtual community' through the development 'of an official ICT vocabulary in Ki'che' and other online resources for other indigenous groups in the region. Gurumurthy (2004: 7) claims that rural populations in the

South have also been marginalized by ICTs because of lack of access and adequate infrastructure and particularly the high cost that is associated with ICT access and usage. Marginalization of women is also common as they are a greater disadvantage due to illiteracy, lack of English language proficiency, and limited training opportunities. These factors further disadvantage women in addition to the burden of domestic duties and restrictions by cultural conventions related to mobility. In developing regions of the world and among developing communities around the word, technology as cultural power may be oppressive in ways that have not been explored as yet. As illustrated by the work of Guenette and Beamish (2005) and Gurumurthy (2004), technology as cultural power may manifest itself in as simple a form as the dominant language of technology.

## Social Impact of Technology Culture

As the foregoing discussion revealed, research over the past decades focused on gender communication, flaming, anonymity and power differentials with regard to general patterns of online communication behaviour. The social impact of technology culture is highlighted in current research (Shachaf, 2008; Horii, 2005; Palomba, 2006) and suggests a trend in acknowledging the technology-culture relationship and its social impact. Palomba (2006: 84) introduces the idea of 'negotiating reality' in cyberspace. that involves (*a*) having an awareness of how your own cultural backgrounds influence your own behaviour and perceptions, (*b*) ability to engage with others to explore assumptions and (*c*) an openness to try different ways of seeing and doing things. This is an area that has become more and more significant in online communication as individuals and groups from diverse global cultures communicate more frequently. It moves past the old debate of gendered communication online and opens a new era in exploring acceptable and unacceptable norms in online intercultural communication.

Horii's (2005) research suggests that there are significant behavioural differences when cultures communicate online. For example, Horii (Ibid.) identified a 'culturally-driven normative system' as a key element of cultural differences. Also, according to him, the 'culturally-driven normative system' refers to conceptions of preferred or desirable standards, not only for individual behaviours in decision-making and communication, but also for organizational practices. The findings of Shachaf's (2008) exploratory study which focused on the effects of cultural diversity and ICT on team effectiveness in an organizational environment revealed that cultural diversity had a positive influence on decision-making and a negative influence on communication. ICT mitigated the negative impact on intercultural communication and supported the positive impact on decision-making. There is a need to find common patterns of culturally acceptable norms online in order to harmonize online communication across diverse cultures.

The third culture notion is one such option which is supported by Raybourne, Kings and Davies (2003) while Kramsch (1993) suggested that it was an issue of finding a 'third space'. Negotiating and identifying commonalities to establish third culture and/or third space is an important development in online communication. The challenge would be to find an approach in establishing third culture and/or third space in virtual space which provides a platform for anonymity and confidentiality. One such strategy is proposed by Palomba (2006: 84) who claims that computer-mediated simulated games offers an ideal opportunity to explore 'prejudice-reduction', particularly because it allows one to explore 'potentially threatening topics in a safe, player-controlled environment'. Furthermore, it encourages online game players to explore different virtual forms of themselves, experience culture shock and regroup their cultural identity during the spaces in between. It also helps them engage in real world experience by shifting between the virtual and real world, while constructing their virtual personas based on their real world personas and to even experience cultural stress tolerance. The introduction of other virtual worlds such as Second Life may have some merit in negotiating cultural diversity issues. However, more research is required to ascertain the merits of online games and virtual world scenarios in enhancing intercultural interactions.

# Conclusion

The power of technology cannot be underestimated in an era when a large number of the world's population is using the media more frequently. Investigating the social impact of technology culture from a wide range of socio-cultural dimensions over the coming decades will reveal some of the complexities of media use coupled with communication behaviours across cultures.

The preceding discussion illustrates the overt and covert ways in which technology impacts our socio-cultural realities. However, it also demonstrates that technology does not automatically empower its users, spread literacy, and bridge the divide (for e.g., in innovation, gender, class and culture). Human mediation is required to channel technology usage in proactive directions so that it becomes a technology of power that advocates for inclusivity, human rights and global community building.

## Chapter 9

# Critical Issues in Intercultural Communication

Islam: 'Not one of you is a believer until he loves for his brother what he loves for himself.' *Fortieth Hadith of an-Nawawi, 13*

## Introduction

This chapter highlights many of the critical issues that have arisen in the discussions in the foregoing chapters. Here, we pull together our thoughts on critical issues in intercultural communication that have been discussed in preceding chapters and we provide a basis for discussion about the complexity of intercultural events that follow in the upcoming chapters. Particularly, we review and highlight the critical issues in intercultural communication that arise out of ignorance and sometimes our reliance on assumptions. We also review the relevance of Klyukanov's (2005) 10 principles of intercultural communication to illustrate how they might explain some of the conflicts and anxieties that we experience in intercultural communication situations. Next, we advocate key principles of global community building that may be applied in all intercultural communication events and encounters in a mutually respectful manner.

# Critical Issues in Intercultural Communication

Critical issues arising within the discussions cross various cultural and political boundaries. First, there is the *commonality of experience across cultures and the uniqueness of each cultural context* that frames the worldview in a significant context. For example, we, as authors, have concerns in common that relate to our experiences as oppressed peoples, immigrants and people who are not privileged by power, status and wealth in the societies in which we live. Another common experience is a deep, painful throbbing reality that our journey to find a place to call home proves to be futile. Despite birthrights in our homelands, our immigrant and permanent residency status and citizenships in new lands, we have no land to call home. In each place where we and our ancestors have travelled and settled, we have remained foreigners, outcasts, migrants, 'boat people' and 'plane people'. However, all our worldviews differ widely and that difference is warmly embalmed deep in our histories, spiritualities and familial relationships and values. This is evident in the multiple and diverse perspectives from which we approach the writing of this book as well as our varied critical perspectives and interpretation of current events in the chapters that follow. Although we seem to speak with one voice, our articulation of voice is distinct. Second, the vast literature review of intercultural communication literature reveals that the *conceptual framework has been developed and presented from the subjugated and dominant perspectives* of master and slave relationships of past centuries and decades. Historical events attest to the fact that after centuries and decades of wars and conflict that enslaved, imprisoned and massacred billions of people, and those who continue to die in the name of democracy, oil and water even today, we have not unchained ourselves from our masters. We are not free people. It is only when we liberate our minds that our souls will be free. Third, we have to *mobilise more people who are committed to the common good* and who believe that all human beings have a right to food, water and shelter (among other basic rights), and who deserve respect and dignity. It is only when we reach critical mass that the global culture will become infused with the true spirit of humanity.

Finally, *building global communities through third culture building* is a noble and honourable goal. However, considering the intercultural conflicts over decades and over the last century, there are enormous challenges in bringing people together in harmony. Gorman (2000) is struck by Tutu's deep faith and positive perspectives on the Truth and Reconciliation Commission while at the same time acknowledging the 'real barriers to true reconciliation'. Tutu's (1999: 120) conviction that *'we can indeed transcend the conflicts of the past, we can hold hands as we realize our common humanity'* must continue to guide us as we aspire toward building a global community. Healing and forgiveness are paths to reconciliation and we should embark on that journey when all else seems hopeless.

## Path to Reconciliation

As we have noted earlier, healing and forgiveness are important considerations in seeking reconciliation among conflicted cultural communities. Many individuals and groups are working for peace with the firm belief that all human beings can live in harmony despite their diverse worldviews. According to Rachel Holmes' review of Tutu's book (1999), Tutu insists that there is a third way to heal a nation's conscience and that for South Africa, the Truth and Reconciliation Commission was the third way. Each nation will have to search for a solution that is suitable to their context and this point was clearly illustrated in the examples cited from Rwandan, South African Bosnian and Herzogovinian history of conflict, and their unique responses to reconcile differences and to heal deep-seated wounds in the last century. According to Gorman (n.d.), 'while Tutu's book looks at national reconciliation through the lens of Christianity, McAleese's focuses on the Christian imperative to forgive through the lens of Northern Ireland's move to reconciliation'.

It is important to keep in mind the critical issues and apply Klyukanov's 10 principles of intercultural communication to lead us to our goal.

# Principles of Intercultural Communication

Klyukanov's 10 principles of intercultural communication have a significant role in global community building and they may be applied as and when appropriate in the global community building process.

The *punctuation principle* advocates the defining of conceptual boundaries through a negotiable process. The *punctuation principle* (2005: 21) suggests that 'people from different cultures define their collective identities by drawing boundary lines between themselves, looking for a mutually acceptable boundary fit' (Ibid.: 20) or an agreed boundary line. The *uncertainty principle* (Ibid.: 43) would help global communities 'constantly search for knowledge of how to interact with one another against the background of uncertainly'. This is framed within an equity approach since the participating cultures have little knowledge about the other and may experience similar levels of uncertainty. However, through a process of negotiation and sharing they begin to disclose relevant information in an effort to eliminate uncertainty as much as possible. The next principle, the *performativity principle* (Ibid.: 71) is important in negotiating meanings through reiterative processes 'whereby people from different cultures enact meanings in order to accomplish their tasks'. This principle provides an opportunity for participating cultures to create and enact meaning that is mutually acceptable and respectful. In intercultural communication events and encounters, participating cultures also have to situate and position or ground themselves and this process where 'different cultures claiming authority for their vision of the world' (Ibid.: 98) is known as the *positionality principle* (Ibid.: 99). If diverse cultures were to hold their own ground in intercultural communication interactions, there would be little hope of building a third shared culture. Negotiating a third shared culture is made possible through the search for common ground in the *commensurability principle* (Ibid.: 126) 'where people from different cultures compare their [cultural] maps and search for common ground, using the same forms and levels of meaning representation'.

Klyukanov (Ibid.: 152) claims that it is through the continuum principle that 'people from different cultures construct a shared and continuous universe while maintaining their different positions'. The continuum principle encourages people to overcome binary thinking by looking through multiple cultural lenses and he admits that this is a complex process. In applying the *continuum principle* 'people from different cultures continuously construct a shared space where meanings are discernable by their distance from each other' (Klyukanov, 2005). Klyukanov's (Ibid.: 179) comparison of intercultural communication to a pendulum is an interesting one because it encompasses the energy expended in the backward and forward motion of participating cultures. At every point of the intercultural communication space, there is constant negotiation, re-negotiation of meaning, and defining and redefining of boundaries. The more complex the intercultural communication encounter, the more frequent the pendulum motion. The *pendulum principle* (Ibid.: 178) defines the 'ongoing and interactive process that simultaneously connects and keeps apart people from different cultures, producing multiple voices'. Most important of all, this principle recognizes that dialogue among cultural communities is an important factor in contributing to the way in which it shapes their shared vision. The next principle highlights the transactional nature of the intercultural communication process. It is common to hear people speak of 'give and take' when negotiating issues on a personal and professional level. The *transaction principle* (Ibid.: 206) creates a *negotiation zone* within which to move 'from positions to interests, in search of an acceptable resolution'. This is the zone within which it is safe to bargain and to offer reasonable choices and options, on the basis of common interests so that a mutually favourable resolution can be reached. It is important for participating cultures to work together to achieve their potential as an acceptable outcome of any intercultural communication event. They have to engage in a synergistic process, which leads to optimal conditions for working together. The *synergy principle* (Ibid.: 232) focuses on the integration *of* 'resources, striving toward an optimal result that cannot be achieved by any culture individually'. Cooperation, collaboration and integration of resources lie at the heart of the synergy principle. Trust, resistance and tolerance lie at the heart of the *sustainability principle* (Ibid.: 258) that requires that 'people from different cultures display mutual tolerance, trust and resistance, sustaining their collective identities and the overall process of their interactions'.

The following critical issues emerge as important considerations in intercultural communication interactions on a regular basis. It is imperative that we take cognizance of such issues once they have been identified and that we respond in appropriate and effective ways to deflate tensions, to avoid offensive behaviours and to promote positive attitudes. Reflection of the critical issues and an exploration of how these might be revisited to one's advantage suggest that they have a significant impact on intercultural communication. Critical issues are carefully reviewed and translated into key principles in global community building. It is envisaged that these key principles will become important considerations in global community building.

# Key Principles of Global Community Building

## Principle 1

*Respect the distinct voice* of individuals and groups from diverse cultures. This is a primary key consideration as a critical issue in intercultural communication. So when approaching the task of building global communities, it is important to keep in mind that diverse cultures are not homogenous simply because they have some things in common. The old literature that focused on homogeneity among cultures must be revisited and critically reviewed in the twenty-first century. The critical question is who advanced those theories and why? How did the concept of homogeneity and essentialization of cultures and groups serve the purposes of a West-centric paradigm in intercultural communication? Particularly, how did that dominant worldview feed the political economy of the past century? These are the critical questions that underlie our daily intercultural communication interactions.

## Principle 2

*Rejection of essentialization of cultures* is the essence of global community-building. Essentializing the experiences of the other is erasing their history, denying their spirituality and obliterating their familial belief and value systems. In the blink of an eye, one has blotted another's identity. First, we need to develop new cultural frameworks that respect and honour diversity among cultures as a way to building sustainable global communities that can live in harmony. Second, it is important to consider the notion of third culture building as the sharing of goodness, cultural virtues and wealth in a way that respects the voice and uniqueness of each participating culture.

## Principle 3

*Conscientizing your inner self* is another critical aspect in advancing the cause of improving intercultural communication and in advocating for justice when an injustice is visible in any form. The Freirean notion of conscientization, cited in Heaney (1995), moves beyond the awareness-raising phase to a critical consciousness level that demands action leading to transformation 'and seeks the liberation of the human will to do so through learning and social action'. We cannot emphasize enough the significance of critical self-reflection and soul searching as a necessary first step in discovering the cultural wealth that other cultures have to offer global community building. The idea is to know yourself first before you attempt to know the other.

## Principle 4

*Interrogate your mental models, stereotypes and prejudices* in order to arrest those demons that prevent you from embracing diverse cultures in open, respectful, meaningful and dignified ways. This principle emphasizes the importance of revisiting your own history, spirituality and family values that shape your world views and create a fair space for other cultures to embrace their own. Keep in mind that history, spirituality and family play as significant a role for other cultures with the same intensity that it holds for you.

## Principle 5

*Build global communities on the basis of goodness* of all participating cultures. Identify the cultural wealth and goodness among participating cultures and begin with short-term goals for engagement and connect these to long-term goals that can be sustained over a period of time. The ultimate goal is peaceful co-existence and this is at the heart of many current global initiatives, like the North Dakota Peace Coalition, which is 'committed to working for peace, human dignity, economic and social justice, and a responsible relationship with the environment. It aims to create a world based on care, compassion, nurture, inclusion, joy and new, bold change.' Another example that deserves a mention is the group of Elders that was convened in 2007 to serve as a group of wise global leaders. The Facing History and Ourselves website educates and informs global communities on various intercultural communication events and encounters and seeks global understanding.

## Principle 6

*Explore third culture building* as a viable option. Map pathways to mutual exchange of perspectives and viewpoints that lie embedded within one's history, spirituality and the familial orientation. Sharing and negotiation across cultures in a fair space are important aspects of third culture building. According to Matoba (n.d.), 'creating a "third culture" is an alternative which honors diverse cultures as threads in the rich weave of a larger whole, without diluting or making less of either'. It is necessary to view third culture building as a reaffirmation of what is good, wholesome and righteous within each culture and to use it strategically in order to collectively benefit humanity as a global family. In this collective global third culture, the histories, spiritualities and families across cultures are connected by the strong bonds of humanity that interweave through our collective consciences, so that we pledge to do what is right and just for all cultural communities.

Key principles in building global communities may be adapted and modified to suit the needs and context of participating cultures. These are negotiable principles and diverse global cultures may want to apply their unique perspectives and creative energies in developing third cultures that benefit all of them and promote compassion. It is evident from the preceding discussion in this chapter and from the overall critical discussion throughout the book that developing harmonious, respectful and dignified intercultural communication is the real challenge. Anyone can develop effective and good intercultural communication, but few can contribute to building a global community on the core values of respect, dignity and harmony.

## Conclusion

Intercultural communication literature is rich and exhaustive with myriad examples of what to do, when and how to engage successfully in any intercultural communication interaction. However, in addition to a range of useful strategies and tips to communicate effectively across cultures, individuals and groups require inner strength and courage to engage diverse cultural communities respectfully in deep and meaningful ways. The warmth and passion with which communities embrace humanity and the sincerity with which they engage cannot be translated into any number of languages because they will bring to the fore their collective consciences.

Principles and practices to improve communication, encourage dialogue, effectively engage communities and resolve conflict abound. However, at the heart of intercultural communication is a human being who requires respect, dignity and compassion. These three qualities are fundamental to every human being's existence and yet, these are underplayed, withheld, trampled, ignored and dismissed in intercultural communication encounters, events and interactions every day. In every language and in every culture, respect, dignity and compassion are recognized as significant factors for peaceful co-existence. Desmond Tutu (2007) has been a strong advocate of peace and his belief in goodness of all people remains unparalleled, as noted on the Elders website, 'despite all of the ghastliness in the world, human beings are made for goodness. The ones that are held in high regard are not militarily powerful, nor even economically prosperous. They have a commitment to try and make the world a better place.'

# Chapter 10

# Intercultural Communication in Practice: Challenges and Barriers

Zoroastrianism: 'That nature alone is good which refrains from doing unto another whatsoever is not good for itself.' *Dadistan-I-Dinik, 94: 5*

## Introduction

The preceding chapters, we provided a theoretical framework or textbook journey of intercultural communication. We encourage you to make use of your critical cultural lens to understand and interpret the varying cultural dimensions involved in any intercultural interaction that you experience and/or observe. Examples of real world events are also presented in the last four chapters for further critical reflection. Responses may vary depending on our historical context, religious orientation and cultural affiliation. The broad overview in previous chapters also explain the concepts of third culture building, differences in values and belief systems, using stereotypes inappropriately and the role of prejudice in discriminatory practices. In this chapter, we make reference to the conceptual frameworks and provide examples of how real life situations of intercultural interactions and events either reinforce our notions and perceptions or completely negate them.

Challenges and barriers that appear and intervene negatively—overtly or covertly—on intercultural communication are highlighted in this chapter. Fostering of cultural respect among diverse communities and valuing and appreciating differences are useful strategies in overcoming obstacles. Next, the discussion focuses on the influences of media, history, culture and religion on our behaviour and interpretation of intercultural interactions and events. The chapter concludes with a discussion on the merits of third culture building, the importance of recognizing voice and identity in the interpretation of intercultural communication events and interactions, and proposals for transitioning to a deeper level of understanding and appreciation on one's own culture and other cultures.

# Challenges and Barriers in Intercultural Communication

Challenges and barriers in intercultural communication arise as a result of the real world events around us and in our daily confrontations of intercultural interactions through personal experience and observation. Furthermore, our rapidly changing world impacted by technology, travel, education and migration brings us in contact with different cultures and co-cultures. In order to survive the challenges of this changing environment, Samovar and Porter (2001: 2) suggest that we tread carefully and with caution when we 'communicate with people whose entire backgrounds, whose very ways of viewing the world and doing things may be completely different' from our own. Often, differences are regarded in a negative light and yet they can be powerfully enriching if we value and appreciate them.

Much of the tension and challenges in intercultural communication encounters can be attributed to the multiple ways in which a number of aspects of intercultural communication—the dynamics of surface and deep culture, differences in values and beliefs, stereotyping and prejudice—are influenced by our own worldview, by the environment and through various media.

## Role of Surface Culture and Deep Culture

The concept of *surface culture* and *deep culture* was discussed earlier using the iceberg metaphor where the tip floats above the water (the surface culture) but the mass is hidden below the surface and thus is invisible (the deep culture). While cultural traits at the surface level are visible and generally easy to recognize, it is more difficult to perceive the cultural traits at the deep level, as they are hidden within several layers of related scaffolds. Sojourners and migrants are often subjected to this challenge of understanding the deep culture. In other words, understanding the deep culture of the host country can be challenging for adaptation, depending on the cultural context or environment. More importantly, ignorance or unfamiliarity of deep cultures can result in 'culture shock' and 'recovery' or adaptation may vary according to how the individual transitions to the new cultural situation (Oberg, 1960).

Indeed, isolation or separateness is not the remedy as cultural contacts are usually unavoidable. While short-term adaptation can be accomplished, it may prove challenging over the long term. This challenge is particularly common with students studying in foreign countries such as the United States. For example, in the aftermath of 9/11 (the terrorist attack on the Twin Towers in New York), female Muslim students in traditional attire are no doubt more conspicuous in the eyes of their American counterparts, who may fail to appreciate that clothing signifies the deep culture of Islam as a religion rather than just a casual manner of dress. The same challenge may be faced by Hindu and Nigerian students who occasionally don their traditional garments to cultural events at college. In other words, ignorance of deep cultures can pose a threat to adaptation for the newcomer. However, this dilemma can be overcome if host environments are more accepting of difference.

To this end, Young Kim (1988) states that receptivity of these environments can play a role in welcoming newcomers but cautions that this practice may vary from culture to culture. Martin and Nakayama (2000) cite the example of US being more welcoming as compared to Muslim societies, which tend to be fairly closed to outsiders. Ignorance of the deep culture of African students has also has negative impact on them. With specific reference to relative status and power between the sojourner and the host group, 'African students often find it more difficult to adapt to US colleges because of racism' (Martin and Nakayama, 2000: 218). As a whole, international students continue to endure this ongoing challenge. In a study, Sandhu and Asrabadi (1994) found that perceived threat and hatred contributed to stress for international students studying in the US. Exploring the level of deep culture and identifying the underlying values and belief systems might assist individuals and groups to focus more consciously on the common threads that bind them.

## Influence of Diverse Value and Belief Systems

An examination and exploration of the deep level of cultural values and beliefs about the way the world *should be* and not the way *it is*, provides an insight into why our worldviews differ. Value and belief systems entrenched in religious orientation, historical roots and family loyalty influence our observations of the world around us and more importantly, how we react and respond to intercultural communication interactions and events. Cultural values influence a vast range of our behaviours including business practice. For example, Japanese business ethics have been examined by management experts in an attempt to enhance productivity in the US (Vogel, cited in Fallows, 1989). A key strength they found is the Japanese belief in the virtue of work itself. This work ethic was manifested in their longer work hours and persistence resulting in better quality products. Fallows (1989) also note this trait in Japanese students' values of education scoring higher on standardized exams than their American counterparts. According to Fallows, this is not to deny that American culture encourages effort in areas such as political campaigns and athletics.

Values and beliefs are also exhibited in the way cultures are inclined towards a more individualistic or collective approach to cross-cultural communication behaviour. Again, a comparison of the business environment of the US and Japanese cultures illustrates this point. According to Martin and Nakayama (2000), cross-cultural trainers in the US report that Japanese and other business personnel often spend years in the US studying English and learning about the country before they decide to establish business or invest. On the other hand, many US companies disregard cultural traits and see no value in providing training before sending their workers abroad while still expecting successful and prompt business deals.

The relationship between humans and nature holds strong implications for value orientations among different cultures. The value system in some societies, such as the US, upholds the supremacy of humans over nature (Neuliep, 2009). This is evident in current programmes in stem-cell research, cloning and birth control methods among others. Indeed, these revolutionary measures create conflicts among pro-life activists, the church and other human rights groups. However, some cultures value and respect nature and in particular the First Nations of America have always displayed such deep belief in the need to create a harmonious environment in which humans and nature can co-exist. In this culture, nature is respected and plays an integral part in the spiritual and religious life of the community (Martin and Nakayama, 2000). Our knowledge and understanding of our own cultural value and belief systems and how we behave within these parameters is key to how we perceive the value and belief systems of other cultures. Ignorance about our own cultures may lead us to make inappropriate judgements about other cultures and in this way we may rely on stereotypes to make sense of our own world and the world around us.

## Effects of Stereotyping

Whitley and Kite's (2006: 6) definition of *stereotype* 'as beliefs and opinions about the characteristics, attitudes and behaviours of members of various groups' is a simple, straightforward explanation as to why we sometimes reaffirm stereotypes of our own culture by fitting into the profiles and representations of ourselves that people expect to see. It is also a good description of what we do on a regular basis, often in subconscious ways to profile others and portray them as we expect to see them. The tendency to stereotype is also influenced by the mass media, schools, families and peers but the effects of stereotyping go beyond the boundaries on one's imagination and can be extremely harmful, derogatory, discriminatory and damaging. Innocent people have been convicted, imprisoned and electrocuted because people relied on stereotyping as their basis of evidence.

Intercultural relationships also have the potential to form, as well as break stereotypes. Friendship and student interactions across cultures in class are evidence of this. For example, negative perceptions of the Holocaust, Middle Passage, Indian Indentureship and the Civil War can often be dispelled by interacting with students whose ancestors have actually experienced these events in history. A current negative stereotype, however, remains the aftermath of the September 11 attacks on the Twin Towers in New York City. The incident, fuelled by the media, has triggered a stereotype of Muslims as terrorists and subsequently, they are profiled by government policies, customs checks and immigration policies. Negative stereotypes can lead to suspicion, fear and hate for ethnic groups and it may take several decades and even centuries to eliminate stereotypes. Almost 10 years after the 9/11 attack in New York, New Yorkers are objecting to the building of a mosque (house of prayer) for Muslims a few blocks from the Twin Tower carnage—known as Ground Zero—in August 2010. This is an example of how stereotyping can lead to prejudice and unfair practice.

## The Injustice of Prejudice

While stereotypes can be both negative and positive, negative stereotypes lead to prejudice. Prejudice often encourages a negative attitude or prejudgement towards a cultural group and can lead to discrimination. According to Samovar and Porter (2001), prejudice includes various levels of hostility when applied to interpersonal and intercultural settings. Martin and Nakayama (2001: 248) describe the following case of prejudice in the healthcare setting:

> A social worker in one of the nursing units was recording information on a patient's chart when she overheard staff members discussing a patient who had recently been admitted to the unit. They were not certain if the patient was Chinese, Taiwanese or Vietnamese. The head nurse called the supervisor of international services, who helped clarify that the patient

was Taiwanese and so needed a Taiwanese-speaking interpreter. As they continued to discuss the patient, one staff member said, "So she doesn't speak any English at all? How does she get along in this country if she can't speak English?" Another staff member responded, "She doesn't need to get along here. They are all on welfare."

These comments underscore the level of prejudice meted out to those who do not belong to the mainstream cultural group. In fact, these attitudes may even go so far as to determine the quality of healthcare that minority patients receive. More importantly, this scenario presents a blatant case of actual discrimination to the extent that the attitudes of the healthcare workers were actually displayed. Further, this case is even more alarming to the extent that nursing and medical schools are inadequate in dealing with purging feelings of homophobia, racism, sexism and other forms of prejudice (Martin and Nakayama, 2001). This scenario demonstrates that prejudice that is unmonitored can continue to fester and can also affect a group of people at a contagious rate. Prejudice in turn results in unjust and discriminate behaviour.

Critical reflections of the 'self' and the 'other' are necessary in order that we respond to such events in a culturally competent and sensitive manner. Intercultural communication in practice is highly challenging when we confront intercultural events in our daily lives either directly or via the media.

## Intercultural Communication in Practice

Various factors affect *our response* to media reported events including our own histories and our spiritual and family affiliations. However, *external factors* such as the medium of reporting and the biases involved in media reporting too play a key role in deciding how we respond. The media is regarded as a primary agent in forming and perpetuating stereotypes. As an institution of tremendous influence in shaping public opinion, media has a responsibility to portray cultural groups truthfully and objectively but this is sometimes not the case. For example, through media lenses, older people may be portrayed as needy and homeless, or perpetrators of criminal activity are generally not Caucasian. The media images of these groups have reinforced negative stereotypes. In this regard, Martin and Nakayama (2001: 42) recount the experience of, Jenni, a student working at a homeless shelter. They claim that Jenni was taken aback by the resilience and adaptability of the children at the shelter which was in contrast to her negative perception of homeless children in general. Further, she realized:

> that it doesn't matter what race you are, you could end up being down on your luck or homeless. It really broke a stereotype for me personally. As much as I hate to admit it, I always thought of homeless people as lazy and usually not white. (Ibid.)

When you read media reports and attempt to interpret and to respond appropriately, stereotypes and mental models affect your judgement; stories told through history come alive; cultural values and beliefs interfere with the 'picture clarity' in your mind; deep bonds with history, religion and family weigh you down; and suddenly the messages received are confused, fuzzy and unclear, if they conflict with your worldview. On the other hand, the messages may be extremely clear because they align perfectly with your own worldview. So you pass judgements from an ethnocentric perspective, holding your perspective as superior. You may condemn and/or condone behaviours, support and uphold the principles that you subscribe to and you may feel elated, frustrated or angry. There may be no closure for you which is uncomfortable, but for some real life events there is no closure.

In an effort to remain positive in any intercultural interaction, one needs to identify common threads and to build upon commonalities, a third culture option, that is based on respect for both cultures.

## Building a Third Culture

The discussion in the previous chapters on the process of globalization suggested that two opposing forces existed in many cultures. Hall (1976), Hofstede (1980, 1991) and Kluckholn and Strodtbeck (1961) are among a number of researchers and scholars in the vast literature on intercultural communication who have identified the opposing cultural forces under various sub-categories, such as high-and-low-context cultures, monochronic and polychronic cultures, individualism and collectivism, high and low power distance cultures, and long-term and short-term orientations. These forces affect and challenge all nations, cultures and individuals in many significant ways in intercultural interactions within which cultures attempt to promote cultural, economic and political partnerships. At the same time, people are pulled apart by nationalism, isolationism, fundamentalism, tribalism, spiritualism and ethnocentrism (Lustig and Koester, 2010). Reconciling these two countervailing forces and values presents a tremendous task in building a global community, but recognition of the strengths of third culture building as a shared and negotiated culture is an important step in building global communities. The dialogic nature of third culture building reflects the notion of intercultural competence that can help reconcile these seemingly opposing values, develop a dynamic equilibrium, integrate values through synergy and enable transformation at personal, social and structural levels (Browaeys and Price, 2008).

Building a global community through the establishment of a third culture satisfies our human desire to make our life meaningful and worthwhile in response to changing environments (Gudykunst, 2005). Particularly, third culture building recognizes the positive synergies across cultures and binds the cultures on the basis of what they hold as common values and beliefs. In Kegley's view (1997: 37), 'Individuals without community are without substance; while communities without individuals are blind'. Kegley suggests that communities and individuals within communities are both strong drivers of community building processes. Community building reflects human expectations and desires about what is acceptable, respectful and just for the common good of all humanity. Staub (1989: 37) concurs that it is part of human desire to 'fully develop and harmoniously integrate their capacities, values, and goals' in deep connection with others and this is another attribute of community building. It is within such a community that they can find their voice and meaning through reaffirming their identities. Gudykunst (2005: 367) points out that 'being part of a community does not mean giving up own individuality'. The third culture is premised on creative and adaptive evolution and interdependence 'in an ongoing process of dialogic communication' that requires people to change to survive within this third culture community (Casmir, 1999: 111).

According to Adair, Tinsley and Taylor (2006), there are two forms of shared schemas in the third culture: identical and overlapping. They state that 'the identical form is that all team members share the same schema form and content with other team members' (Ibid.: 214). They posit that 'teams whose members rank high on high-context communication norms are more likely to develop an identical third culture than teams whose members rank high on low-context communication norms' (Ibid.: 217). They agree that in the multicultural workplace context, the overlapping third culture is more common than the identical third culture. In the overlapping third culture, team members develop a shared understanding of the team's goals, values, expectations and beliefs, but at the same time retain their own, without being forced to relinquish their own cultural and social identities. Cross-cultural synergy can generate positive outcomes and potentials that cannot be realized by any one culture alone.

Third culture building takes expansive and inclusive approaches. It facilitates the optimal use of necessary shared sources for common goals from cultural and ethnic diversity (Casmir, 1992). It respects, encourages and accommodates cultural diversity and differences and views variety and diversity as the basis for excellence (Gudykunst, 2005). It thrives on diversity, dialogues, shared frameworks, norms and worldviews. Participants in third culture building bring with them social and cultural capital that is seen as a valuable asset in international business and in intercultural communication. Third culture building accepts cultural diversity as an asset rather than a disadvantage; it is an enriching experience providing an empowered environment that allows for growth and development of respectful, dignified and just relationships among cultures.

The third culture emphasizes sharing, commonality, mutual interaction, equality, trust and respect but at the same time is open to diversity. Such attributes enable people to interact with original cultures and function as facilitators—a mediating man (Bochner, 1973) and a multicultural man (Adler, 1996)—between cultures. As commonalities are shared and emphasized, members of the third culture are free from bias and prejudice (Lee, 2006: 255). The third culture does not tolerate one-sided adaptation, coercion and cultural domination of one party over the other (Ibid.). It requires participants to adopt the newly emerging core values, reconsider their previously held notions and assumptions, and fight racism, ethnocentrism, prejudice and biases. As Gudykunst (2005: 369) points out, 'the way we think about strangers influences the way we act toward them'. Third culture community building, which is based on an equal footing, is unlikely to be successful if some participants assume cultural, racial, ethnic or linguistic superiority over others.

Casmir and Asuncion-Lande (1989: 294) note that the third culture is open-ended and allows for new information and continuous growth. Gudykunst (2005: 374) argues that, 'openness, not intimacy, is the key to developing community'. It is Gudykunst's view that third culture community building is based on relationships and interdependence. He notes that communication is mutual and reciprocal. If we align our ways of behaviour fit for the third culture, other participants will eventually change their old behaviour to reinforce the relationships. Therefore, he suggests, 'one person can begin a community' (Ibid.: 369). Broome (1991: 241) points out that, 'while one can never become another person, it is possible to erect a structure within the framework of which each other's interpretation of the world or of us takes shape or assumes meaning'. The third culture provides a mutual access to one another where they interact, have dialogues, assert their identity, identify and appreciate the common good and find their voice.

## Interpretations of Intercultural Events: Representations of Voice and Identity

As discussed in Chapter 2, culture and communication influence our perceptions, worldviews, beliefs, expectations and behaviour. We act and interpret the events around us according to the mental map shaped by our culture as 'rules for living and functioning in society' (Samovar, Porter and McDaniel, 2009: 10). It is important to keep this in mind when we attempt to interpret and understand the intercultural interactions and events that unfold around us and that we are exposed to through various media. Our individual and collective interpretations may, in fact, deny voice and identity to others. We learn to read, interpret and understand our cultural map from early childhood through an extensive range of enculturation process, such as family upbringing, school education, mass media, the Internet and interaction with others. Culture, thus transmitted inter-generationally and learned through communication, provides us with social rules to function effectively in our culture. Culture is so abstract that we do not realize its existence until there is a cultural clash when we interact with people from other cultures.

Furthermore, culture gives us a sense of group identity and attachment. Enculturation tends to bring a message home to the cultural members that their culture is superior to any other cultures. Culture therefore is ethnocentric (Samovar, Porter and McDaniel, 2010). Ethnocentrism is a tendency to view one's group as superior and virtuous and one's customs and standards of values as universal and true. From this viewpoint, one may see the 'other' as different, strange, weak, immoral, inferior and contemptible. High levels of ethnocentrism can lead to racism, prejudice, discrimination and bias, which manifest themselves in the linguistic diversity, media, expressions, idioms and words of speakers (Neuliep, 2009). Further, we may be responsible for misrepresenting individuals and groups through misreading the cultural cues within the intercultural events. Our interpretations may be strongly biased toward our own worldviews and our subconscious ethnocentric biases may gravely affect the messages we send and those that we receive. Our voices and identities may superimpose our worldviews and completely discount and dismiss the cultural perspectives of the other voice and identity. Such representation of ethnocentric attitudes and voices reinforce the in-group identity and makes in-group members believe that their culture is the only acceptable one. Extreme ethnocentrism can lead to ethnic cleansing and genocide, as evidenced in Kosovo, Bosnia, Iraq, Georgia, Rwanda, Chechnya, Indonesia, Turkey, Botswana and Sudan.

Another expression of ethnocentricism is the use of a dominant language in the media, education, business, law and government. The language becomes a symbol of power and domination and is perceived to be a vehicle that represents the dominant group's perceptions and experience. The majority group legitimately represents the culture as a whole through linguistic power and minority groups are made voiceless in the cultural hierarchy (Ardner, 1978). Such linguistic power silences other minor cultural groups and reduces them to subordinate muted groups. The muted groups often suppress their ethnic identity and voice in an effort to identify with, fit in and conform to the dominant culture, to avoid being isolated and marginalized. There is often a lack of voice of the marginalized groups and representation in the media. Some minority groups may have their own newspapers and TV channels, but these are communicated in their own languages and do not have any impact on the majority culture. Muted groups' linguistic contribution in writing and speech is minimal, is not valued and is considered inferior by majority culture (Neuliep, 2009). Marginalized groups remain confined to the margins and their voice and identity have no currency in the mainstream life of the dominant society. It becomes necessary to monitor such occurrences and to explore strategies in bridging the divide between dominant and marginalized groups. Understanding and appreciating one's own culture will cultivate an understanding and appreciation of other cultures.

## Understanding and Appreciation of Own and Other Culture

Third culture building requires that individuals and communities continue to challenge the 'us–them' mentality. Cameron (1999) is of the view that in the process of creating a new cultural pattern, which combines elements of each of the participants' original cultures in creative ways, one has to have the ability to appreciate and accommodate cultural differences and integrate them into one's own cognitive mental complexity and framework of thinking and behaviour. Third culture building is unlikely without awareness of one's own culture and the cultures of others. As noted in Chapter 2, our perceptions and personal attitudes are shaped by our culture and we view the world through our cultural lenses. Kim (2001: 207) has rightly pointed out:

Each of us is a product of our cultural background, including gender, ethnicity, family, age, religion, profession, and other life experiences.

Our cultural inventory provides us with valuable insights for understanding our beliefs and attitudes, our values and assumptions. Thus, it is critical that we reflect on the various aspects of our own cultural identity and examine the positive and negative impact on our personal and professional development.

It is ironic that the more intercultural encounters we have, the more we realize how little we know about our own culture, how limited we understand our own cultural perspectives and how eager we are to know more about our cultural strengths and weaknesses.

Third culture building therefore emphasizes the development of an attitude to understand and appreciate our own and other cultures. Adler (1996) and Gudykunst and Kim (1997) make an effort to jump out of one's cultural comfort zone, transcend one's cultural and social heritage (Cameron, 1999) and reach out and accommodate other cultures. To achieve this goal, Corey and Corey (2007: 190) suggest that we must overcome our narrow and limited cultural 'tunnel vision' and avoid the trap of 'cultural encapsulation'. According to Corey and Corey (Ibid.), an encapsulated person with a cultural tunnel vision is defined as the one who:

1. Defines reality according to one set of assumptions;
2. shows insensitivity to cultural variations among individuals;
3. accepts unreasoned assumptions without proof or ignores proof because that might disconfirm one's assumptions;
4. fails to evaluate other view points and makes little attempt to accommodate the behaviour of others; and
5. is trapped in one way of thinking, resists adaptation and rejects alternatives.

Therefore, knowing our own culture and the cultures of others will help us bridge the cultural knowledge gap.

Corey and Corey (2007) remind us that in this third cultural milieu, both cultural commonalities and differences can make the third culture enriching and rewarding. This is in alignment with the Chinese relational philosophy: seeking common ground while reserving differences. The core value of the third culture is cultural synergy. Cultural synergy takes advantage of cultural differences to form a new system within which the third culture operates and to create a novel shared approach that embodies the fundamental elements of their team members' identities and purposes (Adair, Tinsley and Taylor, 2006: 226).

While accommodating differences, it is beneficial to seek a common ground. Human beings have many things in common; for instance, all cultures deal with families, groups, relationships, power, justice, obligations and hierarchies, and so on and so forth. We share many values that are considered universal. Schwartz (1992) in his empirical test in 20 countries based on biological needs of individuals, the needs of social coordination and the survival needs, identified 11 universal values: self-direction, stimulation, hedonism, achievement, power, security, conformity, tradition, spirituality, benevolence and universalism. Seeking similarities that attract third cultural participants in the foreground help them achieve their common goals for the common good by adjusting to the third cultural environment, pushing through perceived limitations, becoming good multicultural facilitators in interpersonal domains, and working in a frame wider than their own personal and cultural values (Adler, 1996; Cameron, 1999; Cooper, Calloway-Thomas and Simonds, 2007; Gudykunst and Kim, 1997).

Gudykunst (2005: 370–72) proposed seven principles for us to follow if we are to understand and appreciate different cultures and to build a third cultural community that satisfies the needs and desires of all people involved:

1. Be committed to the principle of building community.
2. Be mindful to what we do and say.
3. Be conditionally accepting and be open to others.
4. Be concerned for both ourselves and others.
5. Be understanding and appreciate differences.
6. Be ethical and engage in behaviour which is morally right.
7. Be peaceful in our thoughts, words and actions.

Understanding and appreciating one's own culture is the key to embracing other cultures with the respect they deserve. In reflection upon intercultural interactions and events on a day-to-day basis and in the media, one must keep an open mind and view the event from multiple perspectives.

# Conclusion

Intercultural communication in practice presents various barriers and dilemmas for all parties. The authors present third culture building as an alternative to confrontation and conflict. An open-minded approach with a focus on identifying common values and beliefs about all that we hold dear to our hearts—our families, our histories and our spiritualities—is perhaps one way of establishing a harmonious and respectful global community. The third culture is a mutually shared space where members of all cultures can transcend their cultural borders to interact on the basis of shared values and beliefs to reaffirm their unique identities and voices.

Our value and belief systems are deeply embedded in religion, history and family and they surface consciously and subconsciously when we are called upon to identify them through intercultural communication encounters in education, in the media and in our socio-political environments. Our critical cultural lenses together with our social consciences must always be the filter through which we monitor our behaviour, so that we remain responsible and accountable for the consequences of our words, our silences and our actions on the *cultural other*.

# Critical Perspectives in Intercultural Communication Events

**II**

Part II of the book documents and describes real, everyday intercultural communication events that are part of our local and global reality. Examples of intercultural communication events in a global context are presented as examples of real life events that have occurred in the lives of diverse communities around the world. The purpose is to encourage readers to explore their own cultural maps and mental models as they attempt to interpret these intercultural events.

Particularly, the next four chapters advocate a critical reflective perspective of *self* and *conscience* to encourage readers to know themselves first before they judge other cultural behaviour patterns, when they participate observe and engage in intercultural events. Selected news media articles and stories on a diverse range of cultural experiences and intercultural events are presented, so that readers can explore the complexities involved in interpreting messages in a global context. Readers are urged to examine why and how such a large number of environmental, human and other factors affect intercultural communication positively and negatively.

One may want to consider the relevance of Klyukanov's (2005) 10 principles of intercultural communication in the interpretation of various intercultural events and encounters. Different principles may feature significantly in some cases and not in others and this will depend on the context of the intercultural event and one's own worldview. The positionality principle, for instance, may be worth considering as one views media events. It may help understand why and how we subconsciously use the positionality principle and grounding when we interpret the intercultural communication event from the perspective of our own worldview. The basic premise is that cultural knowledge is situated and that every culture defines itself and the world from a certain point of view (Ibid.: 92). This strategy is frequently used and one's mental models, stereotypes and prejudices influence and shape judgements.

Chapters 11 to 14 introduce a range of news media reports for critical review and reflection. This allows the reader to delve deep into his/her *consciousness* and *self* to see how he/she understands and interprets these events. This can be a shocking revelation about one's identity and guilt may surface, making it more difficult to understand the flood of culturally besieged emotions. This may also be a frustrating exercise and for some intercultural interactions there may not be a suitable answer, an agreeable solution and any comfort. There may be no closure, no 'final curtain'. It is important to acknowledge that in attempting to understand the complexity of intercultural interactions that are complicated by human nature, closure may not always be possible; 'it is the attempt to seek understanding that is important'.

Chapter 11 focuses primarily on intercultural events related to the deep beliefs and values of family; Chapter 12 highlights religion as a key aspect in intercultural communication and Chapter 13 reviews historical aspects of intercultural communication. Finally, Chapter 14 focuses on events where cross racial, cultural and gender boundaries are deeply entrenched in historical, religious and familial values.

Here, one is encouraged to consider how the beliefs and values of individuals and groups involved in these intercultural interactions and those who report the intercultural communication event project their different worldviews. Further, one may analyse how these are similar to or different from one's own. We have also included our reflections on selected intercultural communication events to illustrate this point. The reflections are brief, but they are deeply embedded in our historical, spiritual and family affiliations and commitments that we hold and from where we shape our view of the world around us. The purpose of this reflective exercise is to illustrate that each individual and group in any intercultural communication event brings specific meaning based on their individual contexts.

We may not agree with the other worldview but we may come to understand why such a worldview is firmly supported. As our discussion in Chapter 3 noted, this is a result of the deeply-held beliefs and values aligned to one's own worldviews that we pledge our allegiance to—our country and our land—thereby holding on to our histories and our spirituality and defend it to death, as it were, and that we protect our family honour.

# Chapter 11

# Family

Sikhism: 'Treat others as thou wouldst be treated thyself.' *Adi Granth*

This chapter focuses on family as a departure point in our understanding of our own and other cultures' ways of knowing, doing and acting based on their set of values and norms. Family is one of the deep structures of culture and affects the deep-seated values and beliefs of a culture. So it becomes important to critically reflect on how this aspect of culture affects our worldview and how we interpret intercultural communication events that involve family honour and family bonds. Why do we act in certain ways to protect and defend family? What stereotypical and prejudiced notions of diverse cultures lead to positive and negative perceptions of family roles and responsibilities in a global context during any intercultural communication encounter?

The following example illustrates how diverse communities respond to intercultural communication events. Different worldviews, based on the beliefs and values embedded in family, religion and history, affect and influence the interpretation of every intercultural communication event.

---

**BOX 11.1: Prime Minister apologizes to Australia's indigenous people**

19 February 2008

In a speech to Parliament, on 13 February 2008, Australian Prime Minister Kevin Rudd offered a national apology to the Aborigines and the Torres Strait Islanders for their suffering and loss due to Australia's discriminatory policies of the past, such as taking indigenous children from their homes to be raised by white missionaries. This apology not only acknowledges a painful history, but also raises the question, 'How do societies acknowledge the past in order to reconcile the future?'

*Source*: 'Prime Minister Apologizes to Australia's Indigenous People'. Reproduced with permission from Facing History and Ourselves website (19 February 2009).

---

# Mingsheng (China)

As a Chinese reader of the news about the current Australian government's forced removal of Aboriginal children from their families in 2010, I feel stunned. This happened 18 months after the Australian Prime Minister Kevin Rudd made a formal apology on 12 February 2008. This practice in the twenty-first century—which has a history of more than 200 years—is but a continuation of the policy of whiteness under the guise of assimilating cultures by eradicating the so-called threat of indigenous groups. Aboriginal children will continue to lose their identity and become displaced persons in their own land due to such government policies.

# Kay (Singapore)

Stealing is a punishable offence in any civilized society and yet children are stolen from their mothers in the name of 'state care'. On one hand, an Aboriginal child gets arrested and charged for stealing and on the other hand, the government policy enables officials to snatch new-borns and children from their mothers. When will this paradoxical stance of the governments end? Or, are they assuming that another public apology by another prominent politician, probably at the turn of the century, will exonerate them from this continual premeditated crime?

# Prahalad (Trinidad and Tobago)

The disruption of Aboriginal families by welfare workers in Australia can be attributed to institutionalized discrimination by the Australian government against an indigenous people. In this case, it is imposed under the guise of poverty alleviation. This insensitive intervention only serves to perpetuate inhumane treatment to these families and violation of their human rights. It also denies the preservation of a rich heritage of an indigenous community already on the threat of extinction. As nations continue to engage in this practice and impose the hegemony of their dominant cultures on vulnerable minority groups, the rest of the global community, such as the UN and other watchdog groups must become strident in their condemnation.

# Fay (South Africa)

The question for me is why are the children of poor white Australians not taken away from their parents under similar circumstances or are there no poor white people in Australia? Apologies are a good starting point to healing the atrocities committed against a nation, but actions to redress the wrongs must accompany gestures such as an apology. It is when the whole community begins to apologize and to correct such wrongs that there can be hope for a more reconciliatory future.

## Reader's Exercise

Now for each of the following events:

1. Prepare a short initial quick response.
2. Consider how the diverse cultures represented in the event might interpret the event.
3. Examine your worldview with that of the other cultures.
4. What would you propose we do to build a global community that is harmonious, respectful and fair?

---

**BOX 11.2: California apologizes to Chinese Americans**

29 July 2009

On July 17, California passed a bill officially apologizing for discriminatory legislation that denied Chinese immigrants the right to own property, marry whites, or work in the public sector. The *Time* magazine story, 'California Apologizes to Chinese Americans' provides more information about this apology and puts it in the context of other official government apologies that have been offered recently.

*Source*: 'California Apologizes to Chinese Americans'. Reproduced with permission from Facing History and Ourselves website (29 July 2009).

---

**BOX 11.3: Justice of peace denies marriage license to interracial couple**

19 October 2009

Louisiana Justice of the Peace, Keith Bardwell refused to marry an interracial couple. As reported by the Associate Press, Bardwell would not issue a marriage license to Beth Humphrey, who is white, and Terence McKay, who is black, 'out of concern for any children the couple might have'. Bardwell justifies his actions by saying that 'it is his experience that most interracial marriages do not last long'. However, in the 1967 case of *Loving v. Virginia*, the United States Supreme Court ruled that 'under our constitution, the freedom to marry, or not marry, a person of another race resides with the individual and cannot be infringed by the State'. Despite his actions, Bardwell maintains, 'I'm not a racist. I just don't believe in mixing the races that way.'

*Source*: 'Justice of Peace Denies Marriage License'. Reproduced with permissions from Facing History and Ourselves website (19 October 2009).

# Chapter 12

# Religion

Native American: 'Respect for all life is the foundation.' *The Great Law of Peace*

Global communities come together and differ widely in the understanding and practice of their religion. This chapter will focus on religion as an area of peace and love as well as conflict and challenge.

Over several centuries, religious conflict has divided communities on the basis of deeply held religious values and beliefs. In the twenty-first century, we continue to note the extreme forms of religious conflict in different parts of the world. The global media contributes to our information access and understanding of the nature of the conflict but ultimately we bring to each intercultural event our own interpretation of the events. Selected scenarios are analysed and discussed within the context of the preceding discussion on the impact of beliefs and values on diverse styles of communication, interpretations of the messages and multiple environmental factors that affect how and what we communicate in our daily lives. This may promote a deeper understanding of how we view the world around us and how other people view us.

The following example illustrates how diverse communities respond to intercultural communication events. Different worldviews, based on the beliefs and values embedded in family, religion and history, affect and influence the interpretation of every intercultural communication event.

---

**BOX 12.1: When town halls turn to Mecca**

11 December 2008

The story 'When Town Halls Turn to Mecca' outlines the changes occurring throughout Europe as more Islamic immigrants move into communities and as more Muslim citizens and immigrants begin to understand and use political power. In some cases there has been resistance from the European majority, for example some cities in England, Germany, Brussels and Italy have protested building of mosques. Despite some of the contentious rhetoric, there have been many examples of successful collaboration on local levels; the article reads, 'Yet talk of civilisational war in Europe's cobblestoned streets is out of line in one respect: it understates the ability of democratic politics, especially local politics, to adapt to new social phenomena.' For example, mosque built in Brussels, at first protested, is built to include various needed community facilities. In general, the article argues that despite areas of contention, democratic integration, especially at the local level, is happening.

*Source*: 'When Town Halls Turn to Mecca'. Reproduced with permission from Facing History and Ourselves website (11 December 2008).

---

# Mingsheng (China)

It is the Chinese philosophical view that people in this world should live in harmony. A harmonious living, in spite of cultural, religious, social and political difference, is to be achieved through mutual understanding, respect and cooperation. It is through healthy fruitful communication, global community building and cultural exchanges that such mutual respect and understanding can be realized. The concept of harmonization sees differences as assets rather than liabilities.

# Kay (Singapore)

It is very rare to come across something in the news nowadays that relates to social harmony. In fact, it is comforting to see a new world—a harmonious world where people are acknowledged, appreciated and respected for their cultural and religious differences, especially in the current times of tensions caused by racial, ethnic, cultural and religious intolerances.

# Prahalad (Trinidad and Tobago)

Given the recent ethnic tensions between Muslims and their counter-parts in other parts of the world, such as India and Nigeria, this initiative is most laudable in our increasingly diverse world. Cultural sensitivity and understanding hold great potential for world peace and harmony, particularly in plural societies. This is often demonstrated among Muslims, Hindus and Christians in Trinidad and Tobago who participate in each other's festivals and religious events making it a truly 'rainbow' country, as noted by Desmond Tutu and Nelson Mandela who refer to the South African community as a 'rainbow nation'. The unique embracing of Muslims by the local community is particularly significant in the post-9/11 period as it serves to relieve tensions and hostilities towards the entire Muslim community.

# Kay (South Africa)

There is goodness among all human beings and this is only one example of why we should never give up hope on humanity. This is a good story for building global communities and it should be replicated in other ways around the globe. It demonstrates community building at its finest: sharing mutual space, showing respect and embracing humanity with compassion.

## Reader's Exercise

Now for each of the following events:

1. Prepare a short initial quick response.
2. Consider how the diverse cultures represented in the event might interpret the event.
3. Examine your worldview with that of the other cultures.
4. What would you propose we do to build a global community that is harmonious, respectful and fair?

---

**BOX 12.2:  Hundreds killed in Nigeria's religious and ethnic violence**

10 March 2010

The *New York Times* reports that 'a weekend of vicious ethnic violence' left as many as 500 members of a Christian ethnic group murdered and thousands injured in Nigeria 'near the city of Jos, long a center of tensions between Christians and Muslims.' On Sunday, March 7, as early as 3 o'clock in the morning, Hausa-Fulani Muslim attackers 'planted nets and animal traps outside the huts of the villagers, mainly peasant farmers, fired weapons in the air, then attacked with machetes', the *Los Angeles Times* writes. According to the BBC, 'the latest violence is thought to be revenge for similar clashes in January when days of deadly violence in the central Plateau State left more than 300 dead, most of them Muslims'. President of Civil Rights Congress Shehu Sani noted that 'the latest violence strongly resembled the killings in January' when Kuru Karama, a predominantly Muslim village, 'was virtually wiped out, and bodies were thrown into pits and latrines', the *New York Times* reports. Sani visited the villages where the attacks occurred and interviewed dozens of survivors; The *Los Angeles Times* writes. Sani noted that the attacks this year are more sinister: 'they are carefully planned and brutal, with hundreds of villagers killed—including babies, the elderly and anyone else unable to flee'. *Times Online* reports that frightened Christians are leaving their villages in central Nigeria after receiving threats of further attacks from those responsible for the massacre on the 7th of March.

*Source*:  'Hundreds Killed in Nigeria's Religious and Ethnic Violence'. Reproduced with permission from Facing History and Ourselves website (10 March 2010).

---

**BOX 12.3:  A flight is diverted by a prayer seen as ominous**

25 January 2010

Last week a flight attendant on a US Airways Express Flight travelling from La Guardia to Kentucky alerted the cockpit of a suspicious passenger. A 17-year-old observant Jewish boy was beginning the ritual of morning prayer and putting on *tefillin*—'small leather boxes attached to leather straps that observant Jews wear during morning prayers'. To the flight attendant, however, the *tefillin* 'looked ominous, as if the young man were wrapping himself in cables or wires' the *New York Times* reports. The flight was quickly diverted to Philadelphia, where it was met by police officers who went into the cabin to find the boy that the Transportation Security Administration had described as a 'disruptive passenger' and a 'suspicious passenger'. According to Lt. Frank Vanore, a Philadelphia police spokesman, 'It was unfamiliarity that caused this.' The flight crew, never having seen *tefillin*, erred on the side of caution.

*Source*:  'A Flight is Diverted by a Prayer Seen as Ominous'. Reproduced with permission from Facing History and Ourselves website (25 January 2010).

# Religion

13 October 2009

Abercrombie & Fitch refused to hire Samantha Elauf because she wears a headscarf. 19-year-old Elauf is a community college student from Tulsa, Oklahoma. She is Muslim, and covers her head for religious reasons. When Elauf applied for a position at a Tulsa Abercrombie Kids store in June of 2008, she was turned down, and later found out from a friend who works at the store that 'the headscarf cost her the job'. The Equal Employment Opportunity Commission (EEOC) has filed suit against Abercrombie on Elauf's behalf. As quoted in a recent *Time* article, the EEOC's suit 'alleges that Abercrombie "refused to hire Ms. Elauf because she wears a hijab, claiming that the wearing of the headgear was prohibited by its Look Policy," or employee dress code'. Abercrombie & Fitch's position statement maintains that 'under the Look Policy, associates must wear clothing that is consistent with the Abercrombie brand, cannot wear hats or other coverings, and cannot wear clothes that are the color black.' The article states that 'Elauf is suing for back pay and compensation related to emotional pain and anxiety.'

*Source*: 'Abercrombie and Fitch Faces Lawsuit over Headscarf'. Reproduced with permission from Facing History and Ourselves website (9 October 2009).

7 December 2009

On 29 November 2009, over 57 percent of Swiss voters passed a proposed ban on the construction of new minarets in Switzerland. Though 'far-right leaders across Europe have praised the Swiss vote and seized the opportunity to call for similar bans in their own countries', as Forbes.com writes, many people around the world—from Muslims in Cairo to ultra-orthodox rabbis at the Conference of European Rabbis—have opposed the ban, viewing it as racist. As stated in a *New York Times* article, 'the ban has propelled the country to the forefront of a European debate on how far countries should go to assimilate Muslim immigrants and Islamic culture'. Switzerland's justice minister, Eveline Widmer-Schlumpf, conceded that the vote was 'undeniably a reflection of the fears and uncertainties that exist among the population—concerns that Islamic fundamentalist ideas could lead to the establishment of parallel societies'. Award-winning journalist Melik Kaylan offers another side to the argument, pointing out that rather than denoting fascism or racism, the Swiss vote has architectural implications. Kaylan states in his Forbes.com article that 'minarets even when silent tend to dominate a skyline. The Swiss are surely allowed to determine the aesthetics of their cityscapes visually as well as aurally.' Regardless of the motivations, the *NY Daily News* writes that the Swiss ban on minarets has been met with global condemnation, and concern that the Swiss reputation for tolerance has been harmed irreparably.

*Source*: 'Swiss Ban on Minarets'. Reproduced with permission from Facing History and Ourselves website (7 December 2009).

Intercultural Communication

---

### BOX 12.6: Terrorism and media coverage in Mumbai

1 December 2008

Last week in Mumbai, India, coordinated groups of terrorists attacked multiple areas of the city killing including people at a train station, a Jewish Centre, and two luxury hotels. The attacks have left 188 innocent people from many different countries dead. Nine of the ten known terrorists were killed, one suspected terrorist (Ajmal Qasab) was arrested. Currently, much attention is being paid to who is to blame for this attack.

In the confusion and horror over these events, media outlets worked to bring the news to their constituents and tell the story of what was happening. As with many large-scale events of great impact like this one, the different choices in how media outlets report a story can highlight major differences in national perspective and in the perspective of that news source. These events and the impact of the media in relating these terrorist attacks challenge all of us to examine thoughtfully our assumptions and the messages that are helping to form them.

In the case of these attacks, you might start by probing what you current know and believe:

• What do you currently know about the terror attacks?
• What do you think you know?
• What questions do you still have?

Reading from multiple news sites can demonstrate the differences in how media outlets choose to cover certain events. On November 29, 2008, the Christian Science Monitor compared the reports from multiple news outlets.

*Source*: 'Terrorism and Media Coverage in Mumbai'. Reproduced with permission from Facing History and Ourselves website (1 December 2008).

---

### BOX 12.7: A veil closes France's door to citizenship

19 July 2008

In the article, 'A Veil Closes France's Door to Citizenship' published in the *New York Times*, Faiza Silmi was denied French citizenship from France's highest administrative court 'on the ground that her "radical" practice of Islam was incompatible with French values like equality of the sexes'. Ms Silmi was nervous applying for citizenship, but she said, 'I would never have imagined that they would turn me down because of what I choose to wear.' Her husband and children are French citizens and she wanted citizenship as well. The court explained that her citizenship was denied because of 'insufficient assimilation' into France, which made her bring the case to a higher court. This case is the first time French court judged assimilation based on laïcité, France's strict separation of religion and state.

*Source*: 'A Veil Closes France's Door to Citizenship'. Reproduced with permission from Facing History and Ourselves website (19 July 2008).

# Chapter 13

# History

As we know, history forms a very important part of our cultural identities. Who we are and why we feel so strongly about territorial and historical roots of identity is deeply entrenched in the way we experience history. This chapter will focus on historical context, and territorial, regional and national identity.

The following example illustrates how diverse communities respond to intercultural communication events. Different world views, based on the beliefs and values embedded in family, religion and history, affect and influence the interpretation of every intercultural communication event.

---

**BOX 13.1: The new history: Teachers learn to face South Africa's past**

6 June 2008

Recent violence against immigrants in South Africa highlights how the treatment of immigrants is an issue that affects nations around the globe. *The Economist* article, 'Give Them a Better Life' describes the current situation in South Africa. In response to this violence, the South African Institute of Race Relations issued a statement that has implications not only for South Africans but for societies worldwide. They end their statement with the following hope: 'Perhaps one day, South Africans will discover our strength flows from our unity and humanity, not from the colour of our skins or the languages we speak.' Addressing this goal, Facing History and Ourselves is working with

*(Box 13.1 Continued)*

---

educators in South Africa to create curriculum aimed at helping South African students think about their own history, identity, prejudices and the choices they make. *The New History: Teachers Learn to Face South Africa's Past*, published in Edutopia, describes this work and the impact it is having on students and teachers.

Source: *The New History: Teachers Learn to Face South Africa's Past*. Reproduced with permission from Facing History and Ourselves website (6 June 2008).

## Mingsheng (China)

Immigrants are often negatively stereotyped and scapegoated for the ills of the society. Stereotyping can lead to racial discrimination, prejudices and xenophobic violence. What has happened South Africa reflects what is happening in the many multicultural societies, such as New Zealand, Australia, France, the UK and Canada where immigrants are otherwise marginalized and discriminated against. To address these issues, it is imperative to establish global citizen education programme to train people to become global or multicultural citizens and create a third culture where people share and appreciate one another's culture, reaffirm their identities, achieve common goals, treat one another on the basis of respect, equality, fairness, humaneness and dignity regardless of race, skin colour, language, religion and place of birth, and fight racism, prejudice and discrimination.

## Kay (Singapore)

Two things came to my mind when I read the above excerpt:

1. Paulo Freire's inspirational *Pedagogy of the Oppressed* which highlights the significance of liberation of mind and interrogation of one's own dispositions, challenging dominant discourses and enabling those from minority racial groups within a society to be active change agents to make a difference for a better social future and

2. the recent outburst over the 'terrorism' assignment by a high school teacher in Western Australia, where the students were asked to pretend to be terrorists making a political statement by releasing a chemical or biological agent on 'an unsuspecting Australian community'; killing 'the most innocent civilians' to get the political message across; choosing the best time for the attack; explaining their choice of victims; and what effects the attack would have on a human body. Incidentally, the assignment was meant to encourage students to think about terrorism with a different perspective.

The point is, though these two examples are about critical pedagogy, the danger lies as to how educators will put it in practice. I think it is critical that even before one is encouraged to interrogate her/his own dispositions and challenge dominant hegemony, she/he should realize that humans have been on the move from time immemorial and that most parts of the present world were once shaped by past immigrants. I strongly believe that this fundamental self-revelation of historical fact will transcend the prevailing issues on *new* immigrants and the associated derogatory discrimination particularly in South Africa as well as in many *old* settler societies.

## Prahalad (Trinidad and Tobago)

Migratory patterns in search of a better life often leads to tension between migrants and the host community. The situation in South Africa is just another example that is engaging the attention of the international community. The hope offered by the South Africa Institute of Race Relations is consistent with the wishes of Nelson Mandela that humanity must transcend the colour of our skin. In this regard, placing multiculturalism on the school curricula in South Africa is a step in the right direction. Children who are taught to appreciate and value diversity would eventually become global citizens of tomorrow. The role of teachers therefore becomes paramount and South Africa may well be positioned to teach valuable lessons in multiculturalism to the rest of the world.

# Fay (South Africa)

Why is it that immigrant populations in countries around the world forget where they really came from? While indigenous communities have every right to either welcome or reject foreigners on their land, former immigrants are not privileged to make judgements on new immigrants who come to new lands in search of a better life for whatever reason. Immigrants suffer great hardships during their passage to new lands whether they come by boat, plane, camel or ship. Teaching our younger generations about their history and identity is a step in the right direction because knowing who you are and what values you hold close to your heart will bring an appreciation and respect for the other. Sharing of histories and identities must surely bring about a human bond that transcends skin colour.

## Reader's Exercise

Now for each of the following events:

1. Prepare a short initial quick response.
2. Consider how the diverse cultures represented in the event might interpret the event.
3. Examine your world view with that of the other cultures.
4. What would you propose we do to build a global community that is harmonious, respectful and fair?

---

**BOX 13.2: Crossing racial lines: Meeting friends they never had**

---

17 November 2009

Fifty years after they graduated high school, the formerly segregated classes of 1959 in Macon, Georgia gathered together. CNN.com reports 'they returned for a one-of-a-kind 50th high school gathering. The classes of 1959, once segregated by race as well as gender, sat down together for the first time in history.' The idea for such a meeting was generated four years ago 'when a son told his father: "Dad, think about how many friends you missed getting to know".' The father, former head of CNN, Tom Johnson, wrote to graduates of the white boys' school, Lanier, the white girls' school, Miller and the black school, Ballard-Hudson, saying, 'It is a different world today. We no longer are separated, except by personal choice.' Participants felt a common need to come together

*(Box 13.2 Continued)*

*(Box 13.2 Continued)*

to 'discuss the past, while moving forward in the present'. They hoped to set an example for future generations as well as for the elderly in other Southern cities.

*Source*: 'Crossing Racial Lines: Meeting Friends They Never Had'. Reproduced with permission from Facing History and Ourselves website (17 November 2009).

---

**BOX 13.3: No immunity for multinationals implicated in apartheid crimes**

22 January 2010

Several international corporations such as General Motors, Ford Motor Company, and IBM, have been accused of aiding the apartheid regime in South Africa. The Khulumani Support Group is filing a lawsuit in an attempt to attain justice for apartheid survivors. The case is 'grounded on the US Alien Tort Claims Act, which allows foreigners to sue US-based entities for violations of international law', *Legalbrief Today* writes. The international law violation the corporations are accused of is complicity with apartheid, since 'apartheid is considered a crime against humanity'. As *Times Live* states, 'lawyers for those participating in the class action claim that … [these corporations] co-operated in human rights abuses committed by the apartheid regime.' Michael Osborne notes in the *Cape Times*, 'plaintiffs say the multinational corporations provided military hardware and computer technology, and that they collaborated with security forces to put down anti-apartheid and labour protests.' The main question in this case, according to *Legalbrief Today*, is 'whether major multinational giants can be held responsible for the atrocities committed under apartheid'.

*Source*: 'No Immunity for Multinationals Implicated in Apartheid's Crimes'. Reproduced with permission from Facing History and Ourselves website (22 January 2010).

---

**BOX 13.4: An Indonesian artist uses her canvas to unite a nation**

23 October 2008

Grace Siregar in her article tries to unite opposing groups through art in Indonesia. Siregar believes her calling 'is helping the country to vent on canvas instead of at one another'. In her most famous piece, Siregar organized a peace installation in the coconut groves in the city of Tobelo. One of the installation artists, Hans Ririmasse, explains that his piece Your Family, My Family, 'was really about making a statement that we can't be separated by war or poverty or greed or hatred or many other things that have led to the hostility here'. An Indonesian Priest, Father Parrisius Anselmus Jeujanan believes, 'Culture and art have been a media for reconciliation.'

*Source*: 'An Indonesian Artist Uses Her Canvas to Unite a Nation'. Reproduced with permission from Facing History and Ourselves website (23 October 2008).

**173**

# Chapter 14

# Culture, Gender and Race

Other aspects of our identities are fully integrated into a broader range of variables and include culture, gender, nationality, ethnicity, sexuality and race. This chapter will provide examples for discussion of events related to culture, gender and race only to illustrate the points made in preceding discussions in Part I.

The following example illustrates how diverse communities respond to intercultural communication events. Different world views, based on the beliefs and values embedded in family, religion and history, affect and influence the interpretation of every intercultural communication event.

---

**BOX 14.1: Racist speech in the workplace**

---

25 August 2009

Someone in the workplace is vocally racist. A coworker confronts this person, who responds by saying he is 'entitled to free speech' and then becomes 'confrontational, almost violent'. A general contractor wrote about this personal dilemma to 'The Ethicist', a *New York Times* column written by Randy Cohen. The contractor ended his letter by saying 'I am all for free speech, but can't I forbid racist speech on my job site?' Cohen responded in a column titled 'Problem Hires', concluding from both an ethical and legal standpoint that the contractor should 'ban racist speech on the job'. Legally, Cohen writes, 'antidiscrimination law forbids your creating or allowing a hostile work environment'. Though free speech is valued in the US, and employees have the right to discuss controversial issues, the racist worker was not discussing racism, but displaying it vocally—an action that could get him fired.

---

*Source*: 'Racist Speech in the Workplace'. Reproduced with permission from Facing
 History and Ourselves website (25 August 2009).

---

# Mingsheng (China)

Article 17 of the UN Universal Declaration of Human rights stipulates that 'everyone has the right to freedom of opinion and expression'. Article 7 declares that 'all are entitled to equal protection against any discrimination'. These two basic human rights—freedom of expression and freedom from discrimination—complement each other. People have freedom to express their ideas; they expose corruption and fight injustice, oppression and tyranny. However, when exercised unlawfully and irresponsibly to insult, humiliate and intimidate people because of their race, ethnicity, colour, nationality, gender, disability etc, freedom of speech is an offence instead of a right. There are limitations to freedom of speech. There should be a balance between the two rights. Being vocally racist and publicly displaying racism, as indicated in this case, denotes a sense of racial superiority, discrimination, prejudice and violence, and violates the rights of those being discriminated against—freedom from discrimination. In contrast, people have the right to discuss the controversial issues within the boundary within which the rights of others are protected and respected.

# Kay (Singapore)

Sadly, many who are familiar with Article 19 of the United Nations' Universal Declaration of Human Rights about having the right to freedom speech do not seem to know the very first one on the list: Article 1, which advocates that humans are born free and equal in dignity and rights and that all are bestowed with sensibleness and conscience to act towards each other in goodness. Despite the extant rhetoric of multiculturalism and celebration of diversity, racism is still embedded in many workplaces and I guess the workplace mentioned in the above example would attest to this. However, I find Randy Cohen's distinction between display of racism and discussion on racial matters in the example rather ambiguous. How can a discussion on racism be justifiable if it were to take place in an already entrenched racially biased work environment? Wouldn't the discussion especially with the 'vocal' racists like the co-worker in the example inevitably involve display of racism by the same perpetrators? I think the chances of these perpetrators using the distinction to cover up their racial antagonism are more likely than for them to realize that their racially biased attitude is fundamentally unethical. Until the day when everyone unanimously agrees that there is only one race, the human race, regardless of skin colour, country of birth and colour; and that all in this human race are equal in dignity and rights, racists will continue to denigrate the 'racially other'.

## Prahalad (Trinidad and Tobago)

While free speech is enshrined in our constitution, it must be tempered with consideration for diversity and tolerance in today's diverse workforce. Employers should therefore provide their workers with cross-cultural training that would foster harmony in the workplace. These measures would avert potential confrontational situations as well as increase productivity in the workplace. Further, employers need to demonstrate their commitment to racial harmony by stipulating it their vision and mission statements.

## Fay (South Africa)

The 'right to free speech' is only a right and a privilege if that 'free speech' does not harm, disrespect, dishonour and unjustly affect the rights of another human being. The 'right to free speech' carries with it a responsibility on the person who expresses an idea, thought or feeling to ensure that other human beings are not disadvantaged, degraded and discounted as a result of the words uttered and by any actions that follow. Furthermore, it also makes the person accountable for the consequences of the spoken words on the victim and for any harmful actions taken by the person or by anyone else against the victim as a result of the views expressed. Workplaces should be safe environments for employees and employers alike. Respect, dignity and justice should be the key principles upholding the moral fabric of organizations so that organizational communities can work together for their common good.

## Reader's Exercise

Now for each of the following events:

1. Prepare a short initial quick response.
2. Consider how the diverse cultures represented in the event might interpret the event.
3. Examine your world view with that of the other cultures.
4. What would you propose we do to build a global community that is harmonious, respectful and fair?

---

**BOX 14.2: Racism on campus**

2 March 2010

On 15 February 2010, University of California San Diego (UCSD) fraternity students threw a 'ghetto-themed' party called the 'Compton Cookout'. NBC Los Angeles reports that the party was meant 'to mock Black History Month' and the invitation encouraged participants to 'wear chains, don cheap clothes and speak very loudly'. The Detroit Free Press adds that partygoers were promised 'chicken, watermelon and malt liquor'. Students and community leaders in Los Angeles responded, protesting and condemning the event. The Editor-in-Chief of the campus' humor publication 'appeared on UCSD's Student Run Television station on 18 February and called protesters of the controversial party "ungrateful niggers", the *Daily Nexus* writes. Then, on the evening of 25 February, a noose was found in the main library, hanging from a bookcase and facing a window. The Associated Press reports that the student who hung the noose in the library turned herself in to police. She has been suspended and 'is under investigation by campus police for a possible hate crime'; NBC San Diego adds that she could face charges of 'hanging a noose with intent to terrorize'. The Black Student Union (BSU) Chapter at UCSD 'declared the campus climate to be in a "state of emergency", the *Daily Nexus* writes. According to NBC Los Angeles, 'black students comprise less than 2 percent of the university's undergraduates'. Hundreds of students joined a protest on 26 February, both chanting outside the chancellor's office, and sitting silently in a group 'wearing black and listening to fellow students who said that they are tired and hurt after nearly two weeks of racially-charged events', *NBC San Diego* reports.

*Source*: 'Racism on Campus'. Reproduced with permission from Facing History and Ourselves website (2 March 2010).

---

---

**BOX 14.3: Did the Russians' 'Aboriginal Dance' go too far?**

22 February 2010

Russian ice dancers Oksana Domnina and Maxim Shabalin performed a controversial 'Aboriginal dance' routine in the Vancouver Olympics. These world champion figure-skaters revealed their routine a month prior to the Olympics—'a routine that featured didgeridoo music, red loin cloths, white body paint and leaves around their necks, arms and legs', *The Australian* reports. Chairwoman of the New South Wales Aboriginal Land Council Bev Manton said:

> I am offended by the performance and so are our other councilors.... Aboriginal people for very good reason are sensitive about their cultural objects and icons being co-opted by non-Aboriginal people—whether they are from Australia or Russia. It is important for people to tread carefully and respectfully when they are depicting somebody else's culture and I don't think this performance does.

Though they wore fewer leaves, less body paint, and Shabalin changed his bodysuit from dark brown to flesh-toned, their Olympic performance was still controversial. The Washington Post reports that 'some Australian Aboriginal leaders called it offensive cultural theft, with inauthentic steps and gaudy costumes'. A YouTube clip of Domnina and Shabalin practicing the Aboriginal dance a month prior to the Olympics is available online.

*Source*: 'Did the Russians' "Aboriginal Dance" Go Too Far?' Reproduced with permission from Facing History and Ourselves website (22 February 2010).

---

**BOX 14.4: Italy's attack on migrants fuel debate on racism**

30 October 2008

Italy, like many countries in Europe, is experiencing a rise in immigration. Last year there was a 17 per cent rise in immigration to Italy and immigrants now make up six per cent of the Italian population. The *New York Times* article, 'Italy's Attacks on Migrants Fuel Debate on Racism', explains that the rise of immigrants has been accompanied by an increase in violence against immigrants. The most recent attack of an immigrant from Burkina Faso has fueled discussion about whether Italy is facing a 'racism emergency'.

*Source*: 'Italy's Attacks on Migrants Fuel Debate on Racism'. Reproduced with permission from Facing History and Ourselves website (30 October 2008).

---

**BOX 14.5: Boston radio talk show host suspended for his comments about Mexicans**

5 May 2009

According to the *Boston Globe,* 'Jay Severin, the fiery right wing talk show host on Boston's WTKK-FM radio station, was suspended yesterday after calling Mexican immigrants "criminaliens", "primitives", "leeches" and exporters of "women with mustaches and VD", among other incendiary comments.' Responding to the episode, Amparo Anguiano, deputy consul of the Consulate General of Mexico in Boston, labelled Severin's comments 'hatemongering'. Anguiano noted, 'It's not the first time immigrants have been denigrated unfoundedly for being dirty, uncivilized, and bringing in diseases. There's nothing more to say, other than that these statements spread unfounded biases, hate, and prejudice.'

*Source*: 'Boston Radio Talk Show Host Suspended for His Comments about Mexicans'. Reproduced with permission from Facing History and Ourselves website (5 May 2009).

---

**BOX 14.6: CNN readers respond angrily to 'Race or Gender' story**

30 January 2008

In the article, 'CNN Readers Respond Angrily to "Race or Gender" Story', readers respond to the assumption that a candidate's race and gender influences voters' decisions. They raise questions such as: How do aspects of our identity, such as race and gender, impact our voting decisions? Do you think people are more likely to vote for people who look like them or share similar experiences? Should citizens consider race and gender when they vote? What other factors are as important, if not more important, for voters to keep in mind?

*Source*: 'CNN Readers Respond Angrily to 'Race or Gender' Story'. Reproduced with permission from Facing History and Ourselves website (30 January 2008).

---

**BOX 14.7: Talking about race**

28 July 2009

The recent arrest of Henry Louis Gates Jr has brought up strong feelings for many, whether they believe that Gates was a victim of racial profiling by Sgt. James Crowley who arrested Gates outside his own home for 'loud and tumultuous behavior in a public space' according to the police report, or whether they believe Gates overreacted to

*(Box 14.7 Continued)*

*(Box 14.7 Continued)*

Crowley's request for Identification. In her *New York Times* opinion article 'A Lot Said, and Unsaid, about Race', Judith Warner writes that this incident, a mere 'snippet of our culture's ongoing meta-narrative about race' was not just about an ID card and racial profiling, but also about identity, expectation and respect. Our perceptions and reactions to situations are shaped by who we are, which, Warner writes, is in part 'conditioned by our race'. Rather than siding with Gates or Crowley, Warner suggests that we should listen to one another and try to understand one another's perspective.

*Source*: 'Talking about Race'. Reproduced with permission from Facing History and Ourselves website (28 July 2009).

# References

Abdi, A.A. (2008). 'Educating for Human Rights and Global Citizenship: An Introduction', in A.A. Abdi and L. Shultzc (eds), *Educating for Human Rights and Global Citizenship*, pp. 1–10. Albany: State University of New York Press.

Access Economics. (2009). 'The Australian Education Sector and the Economic Contribution of International Students'. Available online at http://globalhighered.files. wordpress.com/2009/04/theaustralianeducationsectorandtheeconomiccontribution ofinternationalstudents-2461.pdf (last date of access: 13 March 2010).

Adair, W.L., C.H. Tinsley and M.S. Taylor. (2006). 'Managing the Intercultural Interface: Third Cultures, Antecedents, and Consequences', *Research on Managing Groups and Teams, 9*: 205–32.

Adler, P.S. (1996). 'Beyond Cultural Identity: Reflection on Cultural and Multicultural Man', in G.R. Weaver (ed.), *Culture, Communication, and Conflict: Readings in Intercultural Relations*, pp. 241–59. MA: Simon & Schuster Customs Publishing.

Altman, I. and M.M. Chemers. (1984). *Culture and Environment*. Cambridge: Cambridge University Press.

Appadurai, A. (1990). 'Disjuncture and Difference in the Global Cultural Economy', *Theory, Culture, and Society, 7*: 295–310.

Ardner, E. (1978). 'Some Outstanding Problems in the Analysis of Events', in G. Schwinner (ed.), *The Yearbook of Symbolic Anthropology*, pp. 103–21. London: Hurst.

Bales, K. (2004). *Disposable People: New Slavery in the Global Economy* (Rev. ed.). Berkeley: University of California Press.

BBC website, 'BNP White-only Policy Must Go'. Available online at http://news.bbc. co.uk/2/hi/uk_news/politics/8485233.stm (last date of access: 12 February 2010).

Beamer, L. and I. Varner. (2008). *Intercultural Communication in the Global Workplace* (4th edition). Sydney: McGraw-Hill/Irwin.

Bochner, S. (1973). 'The Mediating Man and Cultural Diversity', *Topics in Cultural Learning, 1*: 23–37.

Bonilla, M. and G. Cliche. (2004). 'Internet and Society in Latin America and the Caribbean'. Available online at http://www.idrc.ca/en/ev-84529-201-1-DO_TOPIC. html (last date of access: 14 August 2010).

Broome, B.J. (1991). 'Building Shared Meaning: Implications of a Relational Approach to Empathy for Teaching Intercultural Communication', *Communication Education*, *40*: 235–49.

Browaeys, M.J., and R. Price. (2008). *Understanding Cross-cultural Management*. New York: Pearson Education.

Byers, M. (2005). 'Are You a "Global Citizen"? Really? What Does That Mean?' The Tyee website. Available online at http://thetyee.ca/Views/2005/10/05/globalcitizen/ (last date of access: 15 November 2009).

Calder, M. (2000). 'A Concern for Justice: Teaching Using a Global Perspective in the Classroom', *Theory into Practice*, *39* (2): 81–87.

Calder, M. and R. Smith. (1993). *A Better World for All: Development Education for the Classroom*. Smithfield: Alken Press.

Cameron, H. (1999). 'Cultural Shift in Teaching about Values'. Paper presented at the CLWR 7th Annual International Conference on Post-compulsory Education and Training, Australian National Training Authority, Brisbane.

Canaves, S. and S. Oster. (2009). 'Chinese Dialogue on Racism Emerges', *The Wall Street Journal*, 17 November. Available online at http://online.wsj.com/article/SB125830043530149179.html (last date of access: 23 November 2009).

Case, R. (1993). 'Key Elements of Global Perspectives', *Social Education*, *97*: 318–28.

Casmir, F.L. (1978). 'A Multicultural Perspective of Human Communication', in F.L. Casmir (ed.), *Intercultural and International Communication*, pp. 241–57. Washington D.C.: University Press of America.

———. (1992). 'Third Culture Building: A Paradigm Shift for International and Intercultural Communication', in S. Deetz (ed.), *Communication Yearbook*, *16*: 248–407. Beverly Hills, CA: SAGE Publications.

———. (1999). 'Foundations for the Study of Intercultural Communication Based on a Third Culture Building Model', *International Journal of Intercultural Relations*, *23* (1): 91–116.

Casmir, F.L. and N.C. Asuncion-Lande. (1989). 'Intercultural Communication Revisited: Conceptualization, Paradigm Building, and Methodological Approaches', in J.A. Anderson (ed.), *Communication Yearbook 12*, pp. 278–309. Newbury Park, CA: SAGE Publications.

Charles, D. (2008). 'Exams Show Torture of U.S.-Held Detainees', *Reuters*, 18 June. Available online at http://www.reuters.com/article/idUSN18187793 (last date of access: 14 March 2010).

Charon, J.M. (1999). *The Meaning of Sociology* (6th edition). Upper Saddle River, NJ: Prentice-Hall.

Chavez (2006). 'Bush "Devil" U.S. "on the way down"'. Available online at: http://www.cnn.com/2006/WORLD/americas/ 09/20/chavez.un/index.html (last date of access: 18 November 2006).

Chomsky, N. (2000). *Rogue States: The Rule of Foreign Affairs*. Cambridge, MA: South End Press.

# References

Chung, O. (2009). 'China Trade Surplus Shadows Obama Visit', *Asian Times*, 13 November. Available online at http://www.atimes.com/atimes/China_Business/KK13Cb01.html (last date of access: 15 November 2009).

Cogan, J.J. (1998). 'Citizenship Education for the 21st Century: Setting the Context', in J.I. Cogan and R. Derricott (eds), *Citizenship for the 21st century: An International Perspective on Education*, pp. 1–20. London: Kogan Page.

Cooper, P.J., C. Calloway-Thomas, and C.J. Simonds. (2007). *Intercultural Communication: A Text with Readings*. Boston, USA: Pearson Education.

Correspondent. (2009). 'World Bank: FDI in China to Fall by 20 per cent in 2009', 1 July. *People's Daily Online*. Available online at http://english.peopledaily.com.cn/90001/90778/90857/90861/6691150 (last date of access: 15 November 2009).

Corey, M. and G. Corey. (2007). *Becoming a Helper* (5th edition). Belmont, CA: Thomson Brooks/Cole.

Denneburg, J. (1991) 'Nelson Mandela: "No Easy Walk to Freedom". A Biography'. USA: Scholastic Inc.

Dodd, C.H. (1995). *Dynamics of Intercultural Communication*. Iowa: Brown and Benchmark.

Dower, N. and J. Williams. (2002). *Global Citizenship: A Critical Introduction*. New York: Routledge.

Driskell, G.W. and A.L. Brenton. (2005). *Organizational Culture in Action: A Cultural Analysis Workbook*. Belmont, CA: SAGE Publications.

Duncan, M. (2009). 'China Land of Opportunity for Some Young Africans', *Reuters*, 6 November. Available online at http://www.reuters.com/article/lifestyleMolt/idUSTRE5A517M20091106 (last date of access: 22 November 2009).

Earth Charter Commission. (2000). *The Earth Charter*. The Hague: UNESCO. Available online at http://www.earthcharterinaction.org/invent/images/uploads/echarter_english.pdf. (last date of access: 3 January 2011).

Eckert, S. (2006). *Intercultural Communication*. Thompson-South Western: Ann Arbor, USA.

Facing History and Ourselves. (2008). 'CNN Readers Respond Angrily to "Race or Gender" Story', 30 January. Available online at http://www.facinghistory.org/resources/facingtoday/cnn-readers-respond-angrily- (last date of access: 17 March 2010).

———. (2008). 'Prime Minister Apologizes to Australia's Indigenous People', 19 February. Available online at http://www.facinghistory.org/resources/facingtoday/prime-minister-apologizes-au (last date of access: 8 August 2010).

———. (2008). 'The New History: Teachers Learn to Face South Africa's Past', 6 June. Available online at http://www.facinghistory.org/resources/facingtoday/the-new-history-teachers-lea (last date of access: 10 August 2010).

———. (2008). 'A Veil Closes France's Door to Citizenship', 22 July. Available online at http://www.facinghistory.org/resources/facingtoday/a-veil-closes-frances-door-c (last date of access: 17 March 2010).

———. (2008). 'An Indonesian Artist Uses Her Canvas to Unite a Nation', 23 October. Available online at: http://www.facinghistory.org/resources/facingtoday/an-indonesian-artist-uses-he (last date of access: 17 March 2010).

Facing History and Ourselves. (2008). 'Italy's Attacks on Migrants Fuel Debate on Racism', 30 October. Available online at http://www.facinghistory.org/resources/facingtoday/italyper centE2per cent80per cent99s-attacks-migrants-fue (last date of access: 17 March 2010).

———. (2008). 'Terrorism and Media Coverage in Media in Mumbai', 1 December. Available online at http://www.facinghistory.org/resources/facingtoday/terror-mumbai (last date of access: 10 August 2010).

———. (2008). 'When Town Hall Turns to Mecca', 11 December. Available online at http://www.facinghistory.org/resources/facingtoday/when-town-hall-turns-mecca (last date of access: 11 August 2010).

———. (2009). 'Boston Radio Talk Show Host Suspended for His Comments about Mexicans', 5 May. Available online at http://www.facinghistory.org/resources/facingtoday/boston-radio-talk-show-host (last date of access: 17 March 2010).

———. (2009). 'Talking about Race', 28 July. Available online at http://www.facinghistory.org/resources/facingtoday/talking-about-race (last date of access: 17 March 2010).

———. (2009). 'California Apologizes to Chinese Americans'. 29 July. Available online at http://www.facinghistory.org/resources/facingtoday/california-apologizes-chines (last date of access: 10 August 2010).

———. (2009). 'Racist Speech in the Workplace', 25 August. Available online at http://www.facinghistory.org/resources/facingtoday/racist-speech-workplace (last date of access: 17 March 2010).

———. (2009). 'Abercrombie and Fitch Faces Lawsuit over Headscarf', 13 October. Available online at http://www.facinghistory.org/resources/facingtoday/abercrombie-fitch-faces-laws (last date of access: 9 August 2010).

———. (2009). 'Justice of Peace Denies Marriage Rights', 19 October. Available online at http://www.facinghistory.org/resources/facingtoday/justice-peace-denies-marriage (last date of access: 6 August 2010).

———. (2009). 'Crossing Racial Lines: Meeting Friends They Never Had', 17 November. Available online at http://www.facinghistory.org/resources/facingtoday/crossing-racial-lines-meeting-friends-they-never-had (last date of access: 17 March 2010).

———. (2009). 'Swiss Ban on Minaret Building', 7 December. Available online at http://www.facinghistory.org/resources/facingtoday/swiss-ban-minaret-building (last date of access: 22 July 2010).

———. (2010). 'No Immunity for Multinationals Implicated in Apartheid's Crimes', 22 January. Available online at http://www.facinghistory.org/resources/facingtoday/no-immunity-for-multinationals-implicated-in-apartheid-crimes (last date of access: 16 March 2010).

———. (2010). 'A Flight is Diverted by a Prayer Seen As Ominous', 25 January. Available online at http://www.facinghistory.org/resources/facingtoday/flight-diverted-prayer-seen- (last date of access: 22 February 2011).

———. (2010). 'Did the Russian Aboriginal Dance Go Too Far?' 22 February. Available online at: Did The Russians' "Aboriginal Dance" Go Too Far?' (last date of access: 15 March 2010).

# References

Facing History and Ourselves. (2010). 'Hundreds Killed in Nigeria Religious and Ethnic Violence', 10 March. Available online at http://www.facinghistory.org/resources/facingtoday/hundreds-killed-in-nigerias-religious-and-ethnic-violence (last date of access: 8 August 2010).

———. (2010). 'Racism on Campus', 2 March. Available online at http://www.facinghistory.org/resources/facingtoday/racism-campus (last date of access: 20 March 2010).

Falk, R. (1994). 'The Making of Global Citizenship', in B. Steenbergen (ed.), *The Condition of Citizenship*, pp. 127–40. London: SAGE Publications.

Fallows, J. (1989). *More Like Us: Putting America's Native Strengths and Traditional Values to Work to Overcome the Asian Challenge*. Boston: Houghton Mifflin.

Fatehi, K. (2008). *Managing Internationally: Succeeding in Culturally Diverse World*. London: SAGE Publications.

FBI. (2008). 'Hate Crime Statistics'. Available online at http://www.fbi.gov/ucr/hc2008/documents/incidentsandoffenses.pdf (last date of access: 13 March 2010).

Fleming, M. (2006). 'The Concept of "Intercultural Citizenship": Lessons from Fiction and Art', in G. Alred, M. Bryam and K. Fleming (eds), *Education for Intercultural Citizenship: Concepts and Comparisons*, pp. 130–43. Clevedon: Multilingual Matters Ltd.

Fong, M. and R. Chuang (eds). (2004). *Communicating Ethnic and Cultural Identity*. Lanham, MD: Rowman and Littlefield Publishers.

Freire, P. (1973) *Education for Critical Consciousness*. New York, USA: The Continuum Publishing Company.

Garcia, M.C.M. (2006). 'Citizenship Education in Spain: Aspects of Secondary Education', in G. Alred, M. Bryam and K. Fleming (eds), *Education for Intercultural Citizenship: Concepts and Comparisons*, pp. 187–212. Clevedon: Multilingual Matters Ltd.

Giroux, H. (1999). *The Mouse That Roared: Disney and the End of Innocence*. Oxford, UK: Rowman and Littlefield Publishers Inc.

———. (2001). 'Mickey Mouse Monopoly: Disney, Childhood and Corporate Power'. Media Education Foundation Video 52 min. Available online at http://www.mediaed.org/cgi-bin/commerce.cgi (last date of access: 12 March 2010).

*Global Perspectives: A Framework for Global Education in Australian Schools*. (2005 and 2008). Carlton, South Victoria: Curriculum Corporation.

Gorman, M. 'No Future without Forgiveness by Desmond Tutu, and Love in Chaos by Mary McAleese' (Book Review). Available online at http://www.yesmagazine.org/issues/new-stories/book-review-no-future-without-forgiveness-by-desmond-tutu-and-love-in-chaos-by-mary-mcaleese (last date of access: 26 March 2010).

Gregory, R.L. (1998). *Eye and Brain: The Psychology of Seeing* (5th edition). Oxford: Oxford University Press.

Griffin, E.A. (2009). *A First Look at Communication Theory* (7th edition). Boston: McGraw-Hill.

Gudykunst, W.B. (1991). *Bridging Differences: Effective Intergroup Communication*. San Francisco, CA: SAGE Publishers.

———. (2005). *Theorizing about Intercultural Communication*. Thousand Oaks, CA: SAGE.

Gudykunst, W.B. and Y.Y. Kim. (1997). *Communicating with Strangers: An Approach to Intercultural Communication*. New York: McGraw-Hill.

Guenette, L. and R. Beamish. (2005–08). 'Technology and Language: Learning to Say Mouse in Ki'che'. Available online at http://www.idrc.ca/en/ev-86346-201-1-DO_TOPIC.html (last date of access: 12 August 2010).

Gumperz, J., T. Jupp and C. Roberts. (1979). 'Crosstalk: Background Materials and Notes Accompanying the B.B.C. Film' (with T.C. Jupp and C. Roberts), in C. Roberts, E. Davies and T. Jupp (eds) (1992) *Language and Discrimination*. London, UK: Longman.

Gurumurthy, A. (2004). *Gender and ICTs Overview Report*. Brighton, UK: Bridge Publications. Available online at http://www.bridge.ids.ac.uk/reports/CEP-ICTs-OR.pdf (last date of access: 18 August).

———. (2006). 'Promoting Gender Equality? Some Development-related Uses of ICTs by Women', *Development in Practice*, 16 (6). Available online at http://www.siyanda.org/docs/gurumurthy_icts.pdf (last date of access: 20 August 2010).

———. (2010). 'Gender in Community Informatics: Guest Editorial for the Special Issue on Gender and Community Informatics', 14 July. Available online at http://www.ci-journal.net/index.php/ciej/article/view/679/558 (last date of access: 22 August 2010).

Hall, B.J. (2005). *Among Cultures: The Challenge of Communication* (2nd edition). Belmont, CA: Thomson, Wadsworth.

Hall, E.T. (1969). *The Hidden Dimension: Man's Use of Space in Public and Private*. London: Bodley Head.

———. (1976). *Beyond Culture*. Garden City, NY: Doubleday/Anchor Press.

Harraway, D. (1996). 'A Manifesto for Cyborgs: Science, Technology, and Socialist Feminism in the 1980s', in V.J. Vitanza (ed.), *Cyberreader*. Boston, MA: Allyn and Bacon.

Harrison, D. (2010). 'Indian Student Visa Applications Fall by Half', *The Age*, 8 January. Available online at http://www.fisa.org.au/content/indian-student-visa-applications-fall-half (last date of access: 12 March 2010).

Heaney, Tom. (1995). 'Issues in Freirean Pedagogy'. Available online at: http://www.paulofreire.ufpb.br/paulofreire/Files/outros/Issues_in_Freirean_Pedagogy.pdf (last date of access: 22 March 2010).

Henley, W.E. (1875). 'Invictus'. Available online at http://www.poemhunter.com/poem/ (last date of access: 18 March 2010).

Hofstede, G. (1980). *Culture's Consequences: International Differences in Work-related Values*. Los Angeles, CA: SAGE Publications.

———. (1991). *Cultures and Organizations: Software of the Mind*. New York: McGraw-Hill.

Holmes, R. 'Amazon.com Review *Rachel Holmes, Amazon.co.uk*'. Available online at http://www.amazon.com/Future-Without-Forgiveness-Desmond-Tutu/dp/0385496893 (last date of access: 20 March 2010).

Horii, T. (2005). 'Impact of Multiple Normative Systems on the Organizational Performance of International Joint Ventures', (Dissertation). Available online at http://crgp.stanford.edu/publications/dissertations/Horii_2005.pdf (last date of access: 25 August 2010).

# References

Huber, G.P., M.J. O'Connell and Larry L. Cummings. (1975). 'Perceived Environmental Uncertainty: Effects of Information and Structure', *The Academy of Management Journal*, *18* (4): 725–40.

'Human Rights Record of the United States in 2009'. (2010). Available online at http://news.xinhuanet.com/english/2009-02/26/content_10904741.htm (last date of access: 14 March 2010).

Human Rights Watch. (2010). 'Nigeria: Investigate massacre, step up patrols'. Available online at: http://www.hrw.org/en/news/2010/03/08/nigeria-investigate-massacre-step-patrols (last date of access: 3 January 2011).

Ikeda, D. (1996). 'Thoughts on Education for Global Citizenship'. Speech delivered at Teacher's College, Columbia University on 13 June. Available online at http://www.columbia.edu/cu/buddhism/document/tc1996.pdf (last date of access: 15 March 2010).

Jacobs, A. (2008). 'Protests of the spread in China', *The New York Times*, 21 April.

Janzen, R. (2003). 'Five Paradigms of Ethnic Relations', in L.A. Samovar and R.E Porter (eds), *Intercultural Communication: A Reader* (10th edition), pp. 36–42. Belmont, CA: Thomson Wadsworth.

Jones, A. (n.d.), 'Case Study: The Srebrenica Massacre, July 1995', in *Gendercide Watch*. Available online at: http://www.gendercide.org/case_srebrenica.html (last date of access: 3 January 2011).

Kam, C.D. and D.R. Kinder. (2007). 'Terror and Ethnocentrism: Foundations of American Support for the War on Terrorism', *Journal of Politics*, *69* (2): 320–38.

Kantrowitz, B. (1996). 'Men, Women, Computers', in V.J. Vitanza (ed.), *Cyberreader*. Boston, MA: Allyn and Bacon.

Kaplan, R.D. (1994). 'The Coming Anarchy', *The Atlantic Monthly*, *274*(8), 44–76. Available online at http://www.theatlantic.com/magazine/archive/1994/02/the-coming-anarchy/4670/ (last date of access: 13 March 2010).

Kasumagic, L. (2004). Facing History Summer Institute Video, June 15. Available online at http://www.facinghistory.org/video/larisa-kasumagic-talks-about-healing (last date of access: 23 March 2010).

Kegley, J. (1997). *Genuine Individuals and Genuine Communities*. Nashville, TN: Vanderbilt University Press.

Kim, E.Y. (2001). *The Yin and Yang of American Culture: A Paradox*. Yarmouth, ME: Intercultural Press.

Kim, Y.Y. (1988). *Communication and Cross-cultural Adaptation*. Philadelphia: Multilingual Matters.

Knapp, M.L. and J.A. Hall. (2006). *Non-verbal Communication in Human Interaction* (6th edition). Belmont, CA: Thomson.

Kniep, W.M. (1989). 'Global Education as School Reform'. *Education Leadership*, *47*: 43–45.

Kluckholn, F. and F. Strodtbeck. (1961). *Variations in Value Orientations*. Evanston, IL: Peterson & Co.

Klyukanov, I.E. (2005). *Principles of Intercultural Communication*. Boston, MA: Pearson Education.

Kramsch, C. (1993). *Context and Culture in Language Teaching*. Oxford, England: Oxford University Press.

Kubow, P., D. Grossman and A. Ninomiya. (1998). 'Multidimensional Citizenship: Education Policy for the 21st Century', in J.J. Cogan and R. Derricott (eds), *Citizenship for the 21st Century: An International Perspective on Education*, pp. 115–35. London: Kogan Page.

Lagos, T.G. (2002). 'Global Citizenship: Towards a Definition'. Available online at http://depts.washington.edu/gcp/pdf/globalcitizenship.pdf (last date of access: 15 November 2009).

Lee, S. (2003). 'Beyond Cultural Boundary: An Empirical Study of the Third Culture Theory'. Paper presented at the annual meeting of the International Communication Association, Marriott Hotel, San Diego, CA. Available online at http://www.allacademic.com/meta/p112182_index.html (last date of access: 25 February).

———. (2006). 'Somewhere in the Middle: The Measurement of Third Culture', *Journal of Intercultural Communication Research, 35* (3): 253–64.

Leigh, J.W. (1998). *Communicating for Cultural Competence*. Boston, MA: Allyn and Bacon.

Lerner, D. (1958). *The Passing of Traditional Society: Modernizing the Middle East*. Glencoe, IL: Free Press.

Levine, T. and S. Donitsa-Schmidt. (1998). 'Computer Use, Confidence, Attitudes and Knowledge: A Causal Analysis', *Computers in Human Behavior, 14* (1): 125–46.

Lewis, Richard. (2006). *When Cultures Collide: Leading Across Cultures* (3rd edition). Helsinki, Finland: W.S. Bookwell.

Lewis, M. (2009). 'Moving and Mixing: Stories of Migrant Women in New Zealand', in K. Naidoo and F. Patel (eds), *Working Women Stories of Strife, Struggle and Survival*. New Delhi: SAGE Publications.

Li, M. and J.A. Campbell. (2009). 'Accessing Employment: Challenges Faced by Non-native English-speaking Professional Migrants', *Asian and Pacific Migration Journal, 18* (3): 371–95.

Lippman, W. (1922). *Public Opinion*. New York: Harcourt.

Littlejohn, S. (1992). *Theories of Human Communication*. Belmont, CA: Wadsworth/Thomson Learning.

Loden, M. (1996a). *Implementing Diversity*. Burr Ridge, IL: McGraw-Hill Publishing.

———. (1996b). 'Dimensions of Diversity Wheel'. Available online at http://www.diversityhotwire.com/leaders_toolkit/toolkit/definition1.html (last date of access: 18 March 2010).

Lustig, M.W. and J. Koester. (1996). *Intercultural Competence: Interpersonal Communication accross Cultures* (2nd edition) New York: HarperCollins College Publishers.

———. (2006). *Intercultural Competence: Interpersonal Communication accross Cultures* (5th edition). Boston MA: Pearson Education.

———. (2010). *Intercultural Competence: Interpersonal Communi-cation accross Cultures* (6th edition). Boston: Allyn & Bacon.

Madhubuti, H.R. (1990). *Black Men: Obsolete, Single, Dangerous? Afrikan American Families in Transition: Essays in Discovery, Solution and Hope*. Chicago, IL: Third World Press.

# References

Magwaza, T. (2009). 'Experiences of a Black South African Woman', in K. Naidoo and F. Patel (eds), *Working Women Stories of Strife, Struggle and Survival*. New Delhi: SAGE Publications.

Marks, K. (2010). 'Another Indian Student Killed in Australia: Racism or Hard Times to Blame?' The Christian Science Monitor, 7 January. Available online at http://www.csmonitor.com/layout/set/print/content/view/print/272450 (last date of access: 12 March 2010).

Martin, J.N. and T.K. Nakayama. (1989). Mountainview, CA: Mayfield.

———. (2000). *Intercultural Communication in Contexts* (2nd edition). Mountainview, CA: Mayfield.

———. (2001). *Experiencing Intercultural Communication: An Introduction*. Mountainview, CA: Mayfield.

———. (2009). Mountainview, CA: Mayfield

Matoba, K. 'Managing Diversity for Third Culture Building'. Available online at http://www.dialogin.com/Matoba_Kazuma.pdf (last date of access: 24 March 2010).

McIntosh, P. (2005). 'Gender Perspectives on Educating for Global Citizenship', in N. Noddings (ed.), *Educating Citizens for Global Awareness*, pp. 22–39. New York: Teachers College Press.

McLean, M. (1996). *Māori Music*. Auckland: Auckland University Press.

McLuhan, M. (1962). *The Gutenberg Galaxy: The Making of Typographic Man*. Toronto, Canada: Random House of Canada.

McMichael, P. (2004). *Development and Social Change: A Global Perspective* (3rd edition). Los Angeles, CA: SAGE Publications.

Merryfield, M.M. (1993). 'Reflective Practice in Global Education: Strategies for Teacher Educator', *Theory into Practice*, *32*: 27–32.

Miller, J. (2010). 'Movie Review: My Name Is Khan'. Available online at http://www.cinematical.com/2010/02/15/review-my-name-is-khan/ (last date of access: 24 March 2010).

Miller, K. (2003). *Organizational Communication Approaches and Processes* (3rd edition). Boston, MA: Thomson Wadsworth.

Mowlana, H. (1995). 'The Communications Paradox', in *Bulletin of the Atomic Scientists*. Chicago, IL: Educational Foundation for Nuclear Science.

Film Blog. *My Name Is Khan*'s Stand Against Extremism'. (2010). Available online at http://www.guardian.co.uk/film/filmblog/2010/feb/12/india-freedom-of-speech (last date of access: 24 March 2010).

Neuliep, J.W. (2006). *Intercultural Communication: A Contextual Approach* (3rd dition). Thousand Oaks, California: SAGE Publications.

———. (2009). *Intercultural Communication: A Contextual Approach* (4th edition). New Delhi: SAGE Publications.

New Zealand Department of Labour. (2009). 'Employment and Unemployment: December 2008 Quarter'. Available online at http://www.dol.govt.nz/PDFs/lmr-hlfs-dec-08.pdf (last date of access: 6 March 2009).

New Zealand Human Rights Commission. (2009). *Race Relations Report 2008*. Wellington: Human Right Commission.

New Zealand Human Rights Commission. (2010). *Race Relations in 2009*. Wellington: Human Rights Commission. Available online at http://www.hrc.co.nz/hrc_new/hrc/cms/files/documents/08-Mar-2010_14-17-15_HRC_RR_Report_2009web.pdf (last date of access: 3 January 2011).

Noddings, N. (2005). 'Global Citizenship: Promises and Problems', in N. Noddings (ed.), *Educating Citizens for Global Awareness*, pp. 1–21. New York: Teachers College Press.

'North Dakota Peace Coalition'. Available online at http://www.ndpeace.org/ (last date of access: 22 March 2010).

Nunez, C., R.M. Mahdi, and L. Popma. (2007). *Intercultural Sensitivity: From Denial to Intercultural Competence*. Pays Bas: VanGorcum.

NZ Human Rights Commission. (2010). *The Annual Review of Race Relations in 2009*. Wellington: The New Zealand Human Rights Commission.

O'Byrne, D.J. (2003). *The Dimensions of Global Citizenship: Political Identity Beyond the Nation-State*. London: Frank Cass & Ltd.

O'Hair, D., G.W. Friedrich, and L.D. Dixon. (2008). *Strategic Communication in Business and the Professions* (6th edition). Boston, MA: Pearson.

Oberg, K. (1960). 'Cultural Shock: Adjustment to New Cultural Environments', *Practical Anthropology*, 7: 177–82.

Omar, D. (1997). Facing History Human Rights and Justice Conference—Video Clipping, 10 April. Available online at http://www.facinghistory.org/video/dullah-omar-discusses-reconciliation-process (last date of access: 23 March 2010).

Osler, A. (2005). 'Education for Democratic Citizenship: New Challenges in a Global World', in A. Osler and H. Starkey (eds), pp. 3–24. Staffordshire: Trentham Books Limited.

Pacey, A. (1983). The *Culture of Technology*. Cambridge, MA: MIT Press.

Palomba, E. (2006). 'ICT Technologies and Intercultural Issues'. Available online at http://www.formatex.org/micte2006/pdf/82-86.pdf (last date of access: 28 July 2010).

Patel, F. (2009). 'Locating Women's Struggles within an Organisational Cultural Context', in K. Naidoo and F. Patel (eds), *Working Women: Stories of Struggles, Strife and Survival*. New Delhi, India: SAGE Publications.

Paz, J.C. (2004). 'The Internet: An Imagined Object'. Available online at http://www.idrc.ca/en/ev-84512-201-1-DO_TOPIC.html (last date of access: 14 August 2010).

'Reel Bad Arabs Documentary'. Film Review from the Mirror Archives 22 (39) (22–28 March 2007). Available online at http://www.montrealmirror.com/2007/032207/film1.html (last date of access: 18 March 2010).

Rao, S. (1997). 'Jumping on the Internet Bandwagon: Adoption and Uses by Mass Communication Students', *Critique, a Review of Indian Journalism*, 3 (2): 42–44.

Raybourne, E.M., N. Kings, and J. Davies. (2003). 'Adding Cultural Signposts in Adaptive Community-Based Virtual Environments', *Interacting with Computers*, 15 (1): 91–107.

Roberts, C., E. Davies, and T. Jupp. (1992). *Language and Discrimination: A Study of Communication in Multi-ethnic Workplaces*. London: Longman.

Rogers, E.M. (1962). *Diffusion of Innovations*. New York: The Free Press.

———. (1995). *Diffusion of Innovations* (4th edition). New York: The Free Press.

# References

Rogers, E.M. and T.M. Steinfatt. (1999). *Intercultural Communication*. Waveland Press, Inc.

Roux, J.L. (2001). 'Re-examining Global Education's Relevance Beyond 2000', *Research in Education*, 65: 70–80. Available online at http://www.manchesteruniversitypress. co.uk/uploads/docs/650070.pdf (last date of access: 11 March 2010).

Rutayisire, J. (2004). 'Facing History Summer Institute Video', Facing History and Ourselves, Video clipping, 15 July. Available online at http://www.facinghistory.org/ video/john-rutayisire-reconciliation-rwanda (last date of access: 23 March 2010).

Samovar, L.A. and R.E. Porter. (2001). *Communication between Cultures* (4th edition). Belmont, CA: Thomson Wadsworth.

———. (2003). *Intercultural Communication: A Reader* (10th edition). Belmont, CA: Thomson Wadsworth.

———. (2004). *Communication between Cultures* (5th edition). Belmont, CA: Wadsworth/ Thomson Learning.

Samovar, L.A., R.E. Porter and E.R. McDaniel. (2007). *Communication between Cultures* (6th edition). Belmont, CA: Thomson, Wadsworth.

———. (2009). 'Understanding Inter-cultural Communication: The Working Principle', in L.A. Samovar, R.E. Porter and E.R. McDaniel (eds), *Intercultural Communication: A Reader* (12th edition), pp. 6–17. Boston, MA: Wadsworth Cengage Learning.

———. (2010). *Communicating between Cultures* (7th edition). Boston, MA: Wadsworth.

Sandhu, D.S. and B.R. Asrabadi. (1994). 'Development of an Acculturative Stress Scale for International Students: Preliminary Findings', *Psychological Reports*, 75: 435–48.

Sassen, S. (2006). *Territory, Authority, Rights: From Medieval to Global Assemblages*. Princeton, NJ: Princeton University Press.

Schwartz, S.H. (1992). 'Universals in the Content and Structure of Values: Theoretical Advances and Empirical Tests in 20 Countries', *Advances in Experimental Social Psychology*, 25: 1–65.

Scorza, J.A. (2004). 'Teaching Global Citizenship: The Paradox of Competency and Power'. Paper presented at Annual Meeting of the American Political Science Association, 2 September. Available online at http://www.allacademic.com/meta/ p59499_index.html (last date of access: 21 November 2009).

Scupin, R. (ed.). (2000). *Religion and Culture: An Anthropological Focus*. Upper Saddle River, NJ: Prentice-Hall.

Shachaf, P. (2008). 'Cultural Diversity and Information and Communication Technology Impacts on Global Virtual Teams: An Exploratory Study', *Information and Management*, 45 (2): 131–42. Amsterdam, The Netherlands: Elsevier Publishers.

Silva, U. (2004). 'The Social Impact of Information and Communication Technologies at the Local Level'. Available online at http://www.idrc.ca/en/ev-84529-201-1-DO_ TOPIC.html (last date of access: 14 August 2010).

Staub, E. (1989). *The Roots of Evil: The Origins of Genocide and Other Group Violence*. New York: Cambridge University Press.

Shah, A. (2009). 'Poverty Facts and Stats'. Global Issues, 22 March. Available online at http://www.globalissues.org/article/26/poverty-facts-and-stats (last date of access: 14 March 2009).

Shaheen, J. (2001a). 'Commentary in Mickey Mouse Monopoly: Disney, Childhood and Corporate Power'. Media Education Foundation. (Video 52 min.). Available online at http://www.mediaed.org/cgi-bin/commerce.cgi (last date of access: 12 March 2010).

———. (2001b). *Reel Bad Arabs: How Hollywood Vilifies a People*. New York: Interlink Publishing Group.

———. (2006). 'Reel Bad Arabs: How Hollywood Vilifies a People' (Review). Available online at http://www.poptheology.com/2009/11/reel-bad-arabs/

———. (2007a). 'Reel Bad Arabs: How Hollywood Vilifies a People', Media Education Foundation (Film documentary, video: 50 mins). Available online at http://www.mediaed.org/cgi-bin/commerce.cgi (last date of access: 12 March 2010).

———. (2007b). Reel Bad Arabs (Documentary film review via telephone interview). Available online at http://www.montrealmirror.com/2007/032207/film1.html.

Shaver, P., J. Schwartz, D. Kirson, and C. O'Connor. (2001). 'Emotional Knowledge: Further Exploration of Prototype Approach', in W.G. Parrott (ed.), *Emotions in Social Psychology: Essential Readings*, pp. 26–56. Sussex: Psychology Press.

Simmons, S.S. and B.J. Strenecky. (1996). 'Semester at Sea: A Vehicle for Global Education', *Multicultural Review*, 4 (1): 37–40.

Snow, C.P. (1959). *The Two Cultures and a Second Look*. Westford. MA: Cambridge University Press.

Southern Poverty Law Center. 'Hate Map'. Available online at http://www.splcenter.org/get-informed/hate-map (last date of access: 13 March 2010).

Snyder, H. (1995). *Earth Current: The Struggle for the World's Soul*. Nashville: Abingdon Press.

Stacks, D.W., S.R. Hill, and M. Hickson. (1991). *An Introduction to Communication Theory.* New York: Harcourt Brace College Publishers.

Stevens, R. (2010). 'An Important, Lucrative Industry Comes of Age'. *New Zealand Herald*, 25 January. Available online at http://www.nzherald.co.nz/nz/news/article.cfm?c_id=1&objectid=10622027 (last date of access: 13 March 2010).

Streeten, P. (2001). *Globalization: Threat or Opportunity*. Copenhagen: Copenhagen Business School Press.

Studies in Australia website, 'International students in Australia'. Available online at http://www.studiesinaustralia.com/why_study_in_australia/international_students_in_australia (last date of access: 3 January 2011).

Suderman, J. (2007). *Understanding Intercultural Communication* (Canadian edition). Toronto: Nelson Education.

Tannen, D. (1996). 'Gender Gap in Cyberspace', in V.J. Vitanza (ed.), *Cyberreader.* Boston, MA: Allyn and Bacon.

Teo, T. and A.R. Febbraro. (2003). 'Ethnocentrism as a Form of Intuition in Psychology', *Theory and Psychology*, 13 (5): 673–94.

'The Elders'. (2007) Available online at http://www.theelders.org/elders (last date of access: 23 March 2010).

# References

*The Golden Rule.* Available online at https://www.tanenbaum.org/sites/default/files/ TheGoldenRule_English.pdf (last date of access: 16 March 2010).

Tutu, Desmond. (1999). *No Future Without Forgiveness.* London: Doubleday/Random House.

———. (2007). 'Biography'. Available online at http://www.theelders.org/elders/ desmond-tutu#biography (last date of access: 18 March 2010).

Tye, K.A. and B.B. Tye. (1992). *Global Education: A Study of School Change.* Albany: State University of New York.

UMR Research Company. Available online at http://www.umr.co.nz/Contact_Us.php.

Vaugham, G. and M. Hogg. (1995). *Introduction to Social Psychology.* Sydney: Prentice-Hall.

Veal, J. (2007). 'South Korea's Collective Guilt', *Time,* 8 April. Available online at http:// www.time.com/time/nation/article/0,8599,1611964,00.html (last date of access: 27 May 2007).

Walat, M. (2006). 'Towards an Intercultural Frame of Mind: Citizenship in Poland', in G. Alred, M. Bryam, and K. Fleming (eds), *Education for Intercultural Citizenship: Concepts and Comparisons,* pp. 164–86. Clevedon: Multilingual Matters Ltd.

Ward, C. and A.M. Masgoret. (2004). *The Experiences of International Students in New Zealand: Report on the Results of the National Survey.* Wellington: New Zealand Ministry of Education.

We, G. (1993). 'Cross-Gender Communication in Cyberspace'. Available at http:// eserver.org/feminism/cross-gender-comm.txt (last date of access: 16 August 2010).

Whitfield, B. (2004). 'The Indonesian Big Five Cultural Values'. Available online at http://www.expat.or.id/business/bigfive-conflictsofnature.html (last date of access: 21 March 2010).

Whitley, B.E. and M.E. Kite. (2006). *The Psychology of Prejudice and Discrimination.* Belmont, CA: Wadsworth/Thomson Learning.

Williams, F., R.E. Rice, and E.M. Rogers. (1988). *Research Methods and the New Media.* New York: The Free Press.

Wilkins, K.G. (1999). 'Development Discourse on Gender and Communication in Strategies for Social Change', *Journal of Communication,* (Winter): 46–68.

Wood. J. (2001). *Gendered Lives: Communication, Gender and Culture* (6th edition). Toronto, ON: Thomson Wadsworth.

World Cup 2006, GNU Free Documentation License. Available online at http://www. bonjourlafrance.com/france-sport/france-football/french-football-players/zinedine-zidane.htm (last date of access: 23 October 2009).

# Index

# Index

# Index

## Index

**199**

# About the Authors

## Fay Patel

Dr Fay Patel is a lecturer in Higher Education and academic developer at the Centre for University Teaching. Fay received her doctoral degree in mass communication and communication studies at Bowling Green State University, Ohio, USA. She is involved in a number of regional and local higher education projects in curriculum development and assessment, leadership in higher education, internationalization of the curriculum and cultural diversity. Fay has over 25 years of experience as a professor, researcher, academic developer, programme and project coordinator, and leader in higher education in five countries (Australia, New Zealand, Canada, United States of America and South Africa). Fay is South African by birth, a Canadian immigrant and a migrant worker in Australia. Her research interests include the scholarship of teaching and learning, enhancing student learning through teaching development, internationalizing the curriculum, international development and global cultural communication perspectives, diffusion of new media technology, and online research methods and communication. She is the co-editor of *Working Women: Stories of Struggle, Strife and Survival* published by SAGE India in 2009. Fay is also author of *Role of Attitudes and Perceptions in Diffusion of Innovations: Implementation of the Internet and Email in South Africa.* Her forthcoming publication is a co-edited book titled *Diffusion of Innovations and International Development: Critical Perspectives in the 21st Century.*

# Mingsheng Li

Dr Mingsheng Li is a Senior Lecturer in intercultural communication and business communication at the College of Business, Massey University, New Zealand. His doctorate is in the areas of intercultural communication and English language teaching. Prior to his arrival in Australia in 1995, he was an Associate Professor in English language and literature. He was Vice Dean and Acting Dean of Foreign Language School, Yunnan Normal University, China, for over four years. His current research interests relate to international education, migrant studies and teaching English to speakers of other languages (TESOL).

# Prahalad Sooknanan

Dr Prahalad Sooknanan is an Associate Professor at the University of Trinidad and Tobago where he is responsible for the basic communication course. He also teaches at the Arthur Lok Jack, the Graduate School of Business, University of the West Indies, where he teaches the core course in communications to students in the Executive MBA programme. More recently, he has been serving as the local tutor in Trinidad and Tobago for the MA degree in Mass Communication for the University of Leicester's distance education programme. Dr Sooknanan formerly served as a Visiting Assistant Professor at the University of Toledo and Assistant Professor at SUNY College at Potsdam. His research interests include topics in intercultural and mass communication.